Advance Pra:

"Kara-Leah Grant's new book, *Sex, Drugs & (mostly) Yoga: Field Notes from a Kundalini Awakening*, takes you on a roller-coaster ride through Grant's very real and very tumultuous journey through the transformative processes of yoga.

Her growing fearlessness, strength and integrity, which develop through her yoga practices and her willingness to confront her own flaws as well as the shadow sides of others and society as a whole, will impress you. Her unflinching candour and the ferocity of her pursuit of true and full awakening will definitely inspire you!

She doesn't present herself as an expert, an accomplished or model yogini, nor does she hide behind any other facade. She presents the raw reality of her experiences of using yoga in the heroic pursuit of the freedom to come home to her truth, her Self, and find rest in a kind of steady wisdom within herself.

She has taken that wisdom and brought it into her teaching. She's unafraid of walking with people into their shadows to support them bringing the light of Consciousness, the light of yoga, into their heart, mind and body.

Kara-Leah dispels the myth that the transformative power of yoga unfolds with ever expanding peace and love. That transformative power is Kundalini, revered as the great Goddess Shakti, and She is ferocious and unflinching in Her dedication to freeing people from all the causes of suffering. In Her, Grant has found the inner ally she needed to transform her mind, body and relationships."

Lawrence Edwards, PhD, BCN Senior Fellow, LMHC is the President of the Kundalini Research Network, a medical school faculty member and a meditation retreat leader. He is the author of *The Soul's Journey: Guidance From The Divine Within, Awakening Kundalini: The Path to Radical Freedom*, and *Kali's Bazaar penned by Kalidas*.

Testimonials

"Few personal memoirs make for stay-up-all-night reading, but Kara-Leah's latest book defies convention in this and oh-so-many other ways. Her poignantly (and brutally) honest narrative shines the light of truth onto our preconceived notions of psychosis, relationships, and power. It beautifully demonstrates the practice of mindful self-enquiry, not on a yoga mat or meditation cushion, not at the feet of a teacher or guru, but in the gritty, messy, moment-by-moment onslaught of real life."

– SARAH HON,
Conscious Brand Strategist and Yoga Teacher

"What a story!!! Is it Real or not? Kara-Leah masterfully explores the connection between psychosis and spiritual awakening, combining her personal experience with deep insight, feeling and analysis... if you have ever questioned the reality of your experience, wondered what is Real, then *Sex, Drugs & (Mostly) Yoga* is a valuable and much needed perspective."

– RAMA WHARERIMU,
ex-monk, support worker and owner of Soul Jiggle Meditation.

"What we consider crazy and who we label insane is usually determined by someone outside the experience. Here, in Kara-Leah's memoir, we have an opportunity to witness her witnessing herself and providing a much-needed view to how remarkably close awaken-ment can be to so-called insanity. Let's hope with more in-depth inquiries like hers we can learn to discern sooner and support better, and thus grow a culture of more alive, awake humans."

– MELISSA BILLINGTON,
creatrix of MYOGA Freedom & The Amazon Academy.

"Kara-Leah writes with remarkable honesty, immediacy and intimacy. She offers us a glimpse into the very real challenges of spiritual life, and the blessings and unexpected transformation that can come through adversity, losing the familiar, and facing our human vulnerability with clarity and compassion. Her writing, flowing in a stream of consciousness style, takes us straight into our own direct, embodied experience. The humour and candour of her stories and inner unfolding remind us that spiritual life and the search for true meaning have little to do with having everything figured out, being perfect, or controlling conditions. In this day and age, such reminders are precious."

— **Peter Fernando**,
author of *Finding Freedom in Illness*

Books by Kara-Leah Grant

Forty Days of Yoga
The No-More-Excuses Guide to Yoga

Sex, Drugs & (mostly) Yoga

Sex, Drugs & (mostly) Yoga

Field Notes from a Kundalini Awakening

Kara-Leah Grant

Aarohati
Publishing

First published in 2018 by Kara-Leah Grant

© Kara-Leah Grant
Published by Aarohati Publishing
The moral rights of the author have been asserted.
This book is a SpiritCast Network Book

National Library of Australia Cataloguing-in-Publication data:

Author:

Grant, Kara-Leah

Title:

Sex, Drugs & (mostly) Yoga; Field notes from a Kundalini awakening

ISBN:

978-1-730-72742-9

Subjects:

Relationships, Sexuality, Personal Growth, Yoga, Spirituality

---

Editor-in-chief: Feet Banks
Cover Design: Bliss Inventive
Cover Photo: Pete Longworth

Disclaimer:

The material in this publication is of the nature of general comment only, and does not represent professional advice. It is not intended to provide specific guidance for particular circumstances and it should not be relied on as the basis for any decision to take action or not take action on any matter which it covers. Readers should obtain professional advice where appropriate, before making any such decision. To the maximum extent permitted by law, the author and publisher disclaim all responsibility and liability to any person, arising directly or indirectly from any person taking or not taking action based on the information in this publication.

Dedicated to

Jase Boogie Stardust
and all the other shaman, healers, sages
and seers that walk amongst us

Contents

And So We Begin

Prologue

On August 21, 2004, I was admitted to Lion's Gate Hospital's Acute Psych Ward by Dr. Alex Ritchie who stated, "This woman is psychotic. She has very disorganized thoughts and poor insight and poor judgment. She is a risk to herself."

My Canadian fiancé had driven me from our home in Whistler, Canada to the Vancouver hospital late on Friday night – it was 3am when we arrived at the emergency department.

That day, I had slipped into trance, speaking in a different voice and different language. There is no mention of that language in the hospital notes although my fiancé heard it clearly, telling me later it sounded like "ancient Egyptian."

Dr. Philip Severy, who wrote the consultation report on that August visit to Lion's Gate Hospital, saw me the next morning. He noted that I was a "29-year-old woman who has had a first break manic psychosis following heavy use of hallucinogenic drugs including marijuana, LSD, mushrooms and MDMA. She is unable to protect herself, behaving bizarrely, she has no insight and is in denial of reality, therefore cannot be admitted as a voluntary patient."

Like much of the hospital's records of that stay, and the second stay I had a month later after a second manic psychotic break, there are inaccuracies in this assessment.

The "heavy use" reported by the doctor referred to a half a tab of acid, one MDMA pill and a gram of mushrooms I'd had the previous weekend at a four-day music festival. I'd also smoked two joints that week. The "bizarre behaviour" included getting down on my hands and

1

knees in the doctor's office and doing prostrations to the Sun God Ra, in all four directions, while he and my fiancé looked on.

Yeah, bizarre, for sure, in that context. But in the context of being an Egyptian high priestess, pretty damn normal.

Only I wasn't an Egyptian High Priestess – at least, not in this lifetime. I was a freelance journalist, living in a small mountain town in British Columbia and engaged to be married to a Canadian bartender. I'd been there for nearly seven years, waitressing, go-go dancing, writing a screenplay and short stories, and working as a journalist. Oh, and taking shit loads of drugs, it's true, while practicing yoga and meditation.

But at the time of my admittance to Lion's Gate Hospital, I'd been taking less and less drugs, and doing more and more yoga. And I'd been under severe emotional stress in an increasingly strained relationship with my fiancé – a relationship I did not have the skills to navigate.

The verdict from the doctors on my admittance to the Acute Psych Ward was "drug-induced manic psychosis." The reality was far broader than that – the psychological defense patterns I'd constructed during childhood were in overdrive attempting to protect me from the heartache of dealing with my failing relationship. And I was undergoing a major spiritual emergence as my ability to work with energy, know the future, and understand multi-dimensional reality came online. I didn't know it then, but I was clairaudient, clairsentient and claircognizant.

My medical notes allude to this a few times, "Patient admits to having had auditory hallucinosis but is vague about the content." This was my clairaudient ability ramping up. In my discharge notes, it also says, "…was behaving in bizarre ways using her hands to direct energy fields around various people. In the context of all this, it was evident she was losing grip over reality…"

That's true. I did lose grip over reality – even as I was becoming aware of my ability to use my hands to direct energy around people. Something I now do as part of my work, facilitating deep psychological healing and release.

I was discharged from Lion's Gate two days later, on August 23, 2004. My diagnosis at discharge was, "Bipolar Type II with a manic psychosis induced by hallucinogenic drugs".

Dr. Philip Severy prescribed me Olanzapine – to be discontinued after two weeks – and Epival to be taken for several months.

I recall seeing a nurse for a follow-up about two weeks later and telling her I felt great and asking if I needed to continue taking the drugs. She said no, and so I stopped. A week or so later, my fiancé broke up with me and moved out of our house. It was a Tuesday night, and I remember being aware that the next day was my father's birthday in New Zealand.

That's what makes reading my medical notes so fascinating – I have an intimate recall of so many details from that particular time in my life. Yet what is written in the medical notes seems so often wrong, and almost completely devoid of all content of the two experiences of psychosis that I had. Small things; these facts. And yet, they leap out at me when I read the medical notes, "This is wrong, and this is wrong, and that is wrong. And oh wow, look at how my fiancé framed THAT. Oops, ex-fiancé!"

Waking up in the psych ward the second time around was terrifying. Not just because I was committed and unable to leave, but also because the emotional reality of my life finally began to hit me. Except, I was in a locked ward and felt unable to be vulnerable with anyone around me. I couldn't tell anyone what was really going on inside of me – and there was no one there to back me up. I was alone, adrift, and profoundly lost.

This memoir is the story of how I found my way back from that place and reclaimed my experiences through a lens and context that made sense to me.

But this memoir is not "what happened" either. It is just my perspective, at this point in time.

I've written it for myself, and for all the other people like myself, who experience multi-dimensional reality in a world that tells them time is linear and the universe is mechanistic.

It's not.

The universe is a play of consciousness, the One masquerading as the Many.

In Tantra Yoga, the path I follow, one simply dissolves into consciousness. All sense of the individual Self falls away. Yet to have this experience too soon or too fast is fraught with danger, as our psychological constructs need to be dismantled with care and love. Too much knowing, in too short a time, with too little context and grounding can lead to all kinds of apparent mental illness including psychotic experiences. My consciousness was evolving and my psyche was breaking open as part of the healing and growth process.

I know this.

I know it because I have lived this evolution of consciousness all the way into integration and wholeness.

And this is what I want to share with you now.

My story, my 14-year journey, my healing, and my emergence into a being that can navigate the true nature of reality while staying firmly centered and grounded in an apparently-separate sense of Self.

Because while the doctors in the Psych Ward diagnosed me Bipolar II and said I'd had two episodes of manic psychosis, I always suspected something different had happened…

Sobbing, again

Laingholm, New Zealand, 2017

S obbing, again.

No idea why, again.

Another bedroom, another house, another town.

But still, there I am. Same as I always was: fucked up.

And yet not, because there is another aspect of me that is not disturbed by the sobbing. The real me, if you like. The me that holds onto the fucked up one as she soaks her yoga mat with oceans of tears, for unknown reasons, again and again and again.

Am I not yet through this, over this, beyond this? Have I not yet cried enough tears, excavated enough trauma, relived and released enough of my past?

It would appear not. Because however much I wish I were somewhere else, someone else, somehow else... here I am.

Sobbing on my yoga mat.

Again.

* * *

There is a difference though, between the me sobbing now, and the me that was sobbing a year ago, five, ten, years ago, fifteen years ago. And that makes everything somehow okay. Thin sliver okay, but okay enough. That okayness makes it possible for me to hold on while letting go and just allowing myself to rain tears on my mat, again.

Is this even my heart that sobs? Or is it the heart of humanity? Am I crying for all the suffering in the world? All the disconnection and pain which only seems to have amplified and exploded since I was

5

a passionate 11-year-old, angry at the world for hating gay people, for burning the rainforest, for blasting holes in the ozone layer, and just plain angry at how little everyone else seemed to care. Now I'm 42 and nothing has changed out there except that it's worse. Even here in New Zealand, often lauded as 'God's Own Country' – or God's Own for short – we're still decimating the waterways and the fisheries and the forests. We still have over 200,000 children living in poverty. We have families sleeping in cars one step away from joining the homeless people populating our streets while online commenters decry the choices that all these "fucked up poor people" make...

How can one heart hold all this pain? Because it is not just my heart and my pain, it is the heart and the pain of the world. I feel all the world's pain and I haven't learned how to hold it all yet...

* * *

That might not be true.

But it feels true right now as snot drips into my mouth and mingles with the salt of the tears. The back of my neck hurts from the rhythm of my sobbing head, my shoulders are hunched over and there is no one here to hold my 42-year-old self. Sam, eight years old now, is mercifully asleep in the bedroom next to mine, not witnessing this crying episode, although he has witnessed many in the seven years we've been flying solo.

Often, I've known why I've been crying. The pain of leaving his Dad, the terror of being on my own with a child, the heartache of being alone for so many years, the rejection when another man doesn't step up, the overwhelm when juggling single parenthood and a business simply became too much.

And then there's all the personal work I've done. The old pains and heartaches I've dredged up from childhood and beyond, feeling and releasing that which was too painful to feel and release back then. Not just from my lifetime, but from past lifetimes, and from ancestors.

* * *

This sobbing is different though.

This is... I don't know.

There seems to be no rhyme or reason. Oh... I can guess at reasons. The way I felt on the phone this morning when my Dad emotionally blocked my attempts to become part of a family gathering. The ache of a partner who lives 12,000 kms away, moored in the Northern Hemisphere to a child similar in age to mine. The comments I read online from people who don't understand what it's like to live in poverty.

* * *

The wave seems to have passed now. My breath comes in big sighs and there's a cold surge of energy releasing from my torso. Or maybe I'm just cold. September in Auckland might be almost tropical compared to our last place of residence – Glenorchy, in the heart of the South Island – but it's still not cozy in early spring.

I feel the rush of cold radiating out of my body. Witnessing. Observing. Noticing.

Where am I?

Who am I?

I'm not sure I know anymore. There's a chance I've become completely untethered – again. That I've drifted so far away from most people's idea of what constitutes reality that my inner world laid bare could be perceived as the unhinged ranting of a crazy woman. Ah, more tears. Perhaps that is what this is all about... maybe it is grief for the place I find myself.

Grief that I am no longer normal, and haven't been normal for nearly 14 years. That I feel things and see things and appear to know things that are beyond the mainstream ideas of what constitutes reality. Perhaps I cry because I have a sense, even now, that in writing this book, I am forever outing myself and that could mean banishment from society. From the Tribe.

* * *

Or perhaps it doesn't matter why I cry. Only that I allow myself to cry when I am sad without creating a story about what it means.

Breath, more breath. So crucial, so important. That was how I ended up here, sitting on the sheepskin rug I prefer over my actual yoga mat, beside the thin foam mattress filling in for a bed until I can find one within an easy driving distance to this new flat in Laingholm, West Auckland that is within my price range.

I had sat down to do my practice, the same practice I've done every day for the last 585 days. I'm on my way to 1000 Days, consecutively, in the hope that something magical might happen when I get there. Maybe these periodical bouts of sobbing and difficult feelings will finally subside and I'll feel happy again.

* * *

Happy.

Oh wow... I remember feeling happy a few years ago. Wellington, 2014. We were – my son and I – living with a close girlfriend in a huge old wooden villa perched on a hillside overlooking Lyall Bay. Access was via steep stairs, or one of those boxy little lifts that delighted my then 4-year-old every time we rode up. I preferred the stairs, but treated him to the lift whenever I had too much to carry, or too little emotional resilience to coax him into walking up the steps.

It was a Friday morning, that morning I experienced happy. Maybe it wasn't the last time, but it was a memorable time. That happiness was triggered because I'd been out on a date the night before with a sexy man. And it was fleeting, lasting barely the morning.

Why has happy been so damn elusive for me?

Possibly because I haven't valued it much over the years. Derided it even, turning up my nose at the pursuit of happiness as another fool's errand much like the pursuit of a good job, or a good income, or a house in the suburbs. Instead, I was in white-hot pursuit of the only thing that seemed real – truth. Or enlightenment, maybe.

Now, I'm beginning to fear that I've gone too far. That I'll never get to the thing that cannot be got to. And yet, in pursuing that thing, I've forever fucked with my perspective of life. So much so that I can never sink back into the herd and appreciate the small things in life, like

8

a years-old Women's Weekly at the local fish 'n' chip shop on a Friday night before tucking into a feed washed down with a Smirnoff Ice.

And, on top of that, sitting on this sheepskin rug beside my thin foam mattress staring at the altar I set up on the $40 chest of drawers I picked up from the Salvation Army, I'm beginning to wonder if I've simply moved around so much that I am incapable of ever finding home. That maybe, just maybe, I have lost myself forever.

These are just thoughts though. I've trained myself to not put too much store in such thoughts. They sweep through the mind like raging storm clouds and as long as I don't pay them too much heed they'll expend themselves leaving behind clear skies and a still mind once more.

I am here.

This much is true.

I am here.

Crying again, yes.

But here. Breathing. Alive.

Which is more than can be said for the painter of the artwork I'm staring at on the wall above the old dresser – Chili Thom. He died this year, of cancer, an old friend from party days back in Whistler, Canada, when I found plenty of happiness on the back of a pill, or the snort of a line, or the pulse of the dance floor. Maybe I cry for him too, and all he brought and all he didn't have a chance to bring. Because he was even younger than I am now.

I bought that painting when he announced on Facebook that he had cancer. Or that the cancer had come back. I can't remember which. But I just knew then – now. It has to be now. It's titled *Mountains in My Mind*, and in classic Chili style shows puffy, snow-weighted trees in the foreground leading into roiling pink and blue tinted clouds covering sweeping mountain vistas.

I lived in that mountain paradise for seven years, and it was magic. I'd dreamed of owning a Chili Thom since the days when my Australian boyfriend and I used to drink a couple of litres of hot sake over a three-hour sushi dinner while staring at a whopping big painting claiming space on the entire restaurant wall – yes, one of Chili's. He was a waiter at the restaurant, Sushi Village. And, like many of the tribe I hung with, talented and creative as all hell. I would stare at Chili's painting through the increasing blur of sake, mitigated when necessary by lines of blow sucked up in the toilets down the hall, and I vowed that one day, when I had a house big enough and money in the bank, I would buy that painting.

When Chili announced he had cancer, I had neither the house, nor the money. And shipping something that big – metres by metres all the way to New Zealand, was not an option. But I jumped on his website, and I moved some money around, and I used my overdraft to buy the biggest damn Chili Thom I could afford. Which wasn't big. 60cms by 90cms. But I bought it, finally fulfilling a dream I'd cherished for 15 years, just not in the style that I'd envisioned. Of course, I never envisioned back in those sake-fuelled days that Chili would get stomach cancer and die at the age of 40.

The last time I remember seeing him was on a dance floor at a four-day festival. I was high on acid. Likely he was high on something too. It was Sunday, and daytime, and we were all at the beach stage, beside the river, dancing up a storm to most excellent beats. He was still married then to Kelsey, an Australian fairy princess drowning in creativity of her own, with a mane of red hair and freckles to match.

I remember watching him and Kelsey, and the crowd of friends around them, and feeling like they were the mother and father of us all, or the King and Queen... that in some way, they nourished and sustained every one of us through their off-beat, quirky creativity that knew no bounds and burst out of them in all directions in unexpected ways. That they were the glue for something far bigger than just this dance floor party. And so, armed with this acid-deep understanding of the power they wielded and the role they played, I scuttled off to find them some nourishment – something to eat and drink, something to take care of them, in the way that they took care of everybody else.

Yeah, I was fucked up on acid.

And it was all true.

Chili was the glue, in so many ways, for so many people. He lived more in his 40 years than most people live in lifetimes, not giving a fuck and splattering his enthusiastic, creative, crazy, wild ways in every direction.

I may have never seen Chili again, after bringing him that food.

I don't remember. That acid trip at Shambhala Music Festival spiralled out into a psychotic episode that landed me in a psych ward with psychosis. A month later, my fiancé dumped me, triggering a second episode and a second visit to Lion's Gate Hospital Psych Ward in nearby Vancouver. It guaranteed that the only trip I was taking for the next while was a one-way trip home to New Zealand, exactly eight years after I'd left Auckland and a promising journalist career for my big OE (Overseas Experience).

I was 29 years old.

I'd just spent the happiest time of my life living in Whistler, BC with a community of people I adored in a town I loved.

They were my tribe – the first time I'd felt completely accepted for who I was, and completely free to be who I was.

OK, the drugs had a lot to do with feeling free and feeling accepted and loved…

But those feelings were real. My tribe was real. The wild and crazy and creative times we had were real. MY fiancé was real – he who I loved so fucking much.

And it was all gone.

And it felt like I was all gone, too. My audacious, powerful, joyous, light and free self.

I was gone.

Nothing was left.

Nothing but debt, a broken heart, and a broken mind.

Oh, and a diagnosis of bipolar disorder. That too. I had that. Although, technically, you can't 'diagnose' bipolar disorder. Technically, what I had was a classification. Because bipolar disorder is the observation of a collection of behaviours grouped together under a name.

But how did this happen? How did I – a middle-class Pakeha (white) woman from Dunedin New Zealand, who was runner-up to Dux at high school and a talented writer – end up going crazy? Surely my childhood wasn't that fucked up? Surely I wasn't that fucked up?

* * *

Laingholm, 2017

The waves of sobbing have passed now.
I feel okay.
Fragile. But okay.
Now, I can practice.
My mind seems still too.
I like this – the stillness.
I can rest here.
It may not be happy, but happiness is fleeting.
Stillness, now… stillness is forever.

When Home is Not Home

Laingholm, 2017

I breathe.
And watch the shadows dance on the wall behind the spider plant harvested from one I left behind in Glenorchy a month ago.

Here in Auckland, the power is out.

Unplanned.

We have candles, my laptop is at 95% and my phone is plugged into the laptop.

No sobbing tonight. No happiness neither. A calmness, yet something stirs beneath the surface. All is not right. Wait – not true. Right and wrong are but constructs of the conditioned mind. Emotion lurks. That's more accurate. These emotions spilled out – unplanned – this morning when I sat across the wooden dining room table from my new flatmate Georgi. It's her table, her house, her space and her place. And that makes me feel vulnerable. I'm fearful (unconsciously paranoid?) that she could ask us to leave at any moment. So when she asked to have a word with me, the fear leapt up into my throat.

It's not irrational. We were asked to leave a house only three weeks ago. Then, I was relieved, as it wasn't the right house, or situation for us.

But here, now… I love this place. It feels… right.

I don't want to leave.

I'm afraid of leaving.

Housing insecurity, right there. Vulnerability. Ah – vulnerability. That's something I've spent the last few years working my way around, edging towards being able to feel, able to be – not just on screen or in words, not just on the phone, but in person, with real live people… vulnerable.

* * *

13

At the table, I sit across from Georgi, and she shares with grace and skill what is in her heart. A child's game, left out. Jam all over the table. Game left on the table in the puddle of jam. Sam's breakfast. Or what's left of it. I'd missed the mess in the morning school dash, more concerned with leaving in time to walk and getting a load of washing started than checking up on Sam.

I'm grateful that Georgi is able to share quickly what upsets her, and I am aghast as I apologise – but not surprised – when I burst into tears.

"I lived in spaces before where it felt like I was walking on eggshells – uncertain of what was okay and not okay and when I might make someone angry without knowing."

Listening to myself speak, and cry, I realise a truth I'd never known. Of how vulnerable I've felt at different times in my life, in various houses around the world. Dunedin, Oamaru, Auckland, London, Chamonix, Sydney, Melbourne, Whistler, Maui... how many times was I afraid and vulnerable and completely unconscious of it?

Now, I'm not unconscious. Now, I feel it. It washes through me in a gulping wave of tears and I allow it to come. The initial embarrassment at feeling passes as I allow myself to simply share what I feel.

Because being able to feel and express with ease the truth of one's moment to moment existence?

That's gold. Fucking gold.

It's the space I hold on the retreats I lead both here in New Zealand and internationally. We sit in circle, the participants and myself, and I hold space for people to take off the masks and the identities and the roles they play so they can simply show up as they are. Feel what they feel. Reveal their hearts.

Nothing anybody feels, thinks, or has done can faze me. Not anymore.

It's powerful work, and it's work that psychosis and my recovery have intimately trained me for.

* * *

Queenstown, 2004

My mum, eyeing me warily but with love, picked me up from Queenstown Airport when I flew back from Vancouver on October 5th, 2004, post-psychosis. I hesitate to say home, because it didn't feel like I was coming home. Whistler was my home. Canada was my home. New Zealand was the place I'd left behind, and the family I'd left behind. New Zealand held the psychological patterning I'd tried to outrun and leave behind too. But here I was, again.

It had been eight years exactly since I'd flown out to London – a Venus cycle. Relevant? Not relevant? In those days, I looked for patterns everywhere – a classic safety mechanism hard-wired into the human condition. Recognizable patterns offer a way of keeping safe, the known and familiar. Possibly that eight-year cycle between leaving and returning means nothing but it was a pattern that was to repeat itself again, and again.

I'd been stopped at Customs in Auckland – my bought-at-the-last-minute ticket had raised suspicions. The young Islander man charged with searching my belongings was confronted with a pile of G-strings on the very top of my bag, and pills…bottles of pills.

"Prescriptions," I explained, digging out the paperwork from my handbag. "I've just come from the psych ward. It's Epival and Olanzapine. An anti-psychotic."

He zipped my bag up again. No need to dig further. I was on my way. Medications, G-strings and all.

And a pile of cheap Ecstasy pills to on-sell to Kiwi ravers.

Joking.

Like for real, joking.

There were no other drugs in my bags or on my person. My shattered psyche meant recreational drugs were off-limits. My new reality – was all about the pharmaceuticals, which I had no intention of staying on longer than required. Family experience with the damage lithium could do to one's brain had led me to refuse that particular prescription, but I knew I had to say yes to something or they wouldn't have let me out of Lion's Gate Acute Psych Ward. So I said yes to Epival.

For now.

Until I figured out what had really happened to me, because surely it wasn't just psychosis.

* * *

I was shocked when my mum burst into tears as I walked through Queenstown Arrivals.

Why was she crying? I couldn't fathom then what she'd been through – half a world away from her eldest daughter, a late-night phone call informing her I'd been admitted, – and then committed, – to a psych ward. She'd been prepared to come over and get me, especially after a desperate call from my fiancé – now ex-fiancé – saying he couldn't cope. But I'd dissuaded her. I didn't want her to spend the money and, psychotic or not, I was quite capable of making it home by myself.

I don't remember the rest of our greeting, or the 45-minute drive up Lake Wakatipu to Glenorchy township, a tiny hamlet at the top of the lake with population 400.

What does stand out is my terror at being vulnerable in front of my Mum.

I. Could. Not. Do. It.

Other people feel safe and protected when they are with their mother. Me, I was terrified of being emotional. Of being real. Of revealing my heart. And I'm still not sure why. Even now, thirteen years later, that pattern has yet to fully unwind.

Whatever I was feeling after flying across the world, after leaving behind my fiancé, after being forced to abandon my friends and my town and my life... I stuffed it all down and held it all in and when I walked into the school house Mum rented as the principal of Glenorchy School... I headed straight for the bathroom, jumped in the shower, and sobbed my heart out under the safety and cover of the falling water.

Never had I felt more disconnected, alone and isolated. Never so totally lost.

I feel her now, that 29-year-old woman. Girl really... Her entire world had shattered in a way that seemed beyond the pale.

Psychosis.

16

Bipolar disorder.

Mentally ill.

Yet that's not where my suffering was focused. It was the loss of my community and my place and my purpose and my service that hurt most.

The loss of my tribe.

In Whistler, I had found a niche where I belonged. I felt connected there, worthy, as if I was someone doing something, going somewhere.

Now, that was all gone.

Instead I was back, imprisoned inside the walls of my childhood, the prison of expectations about who I was meant to be, who I should be, and who I had to be if I wanted to be accepted and loved.

I felt invisible again.

* * *

All these years later, I still feel that loss – of community and place. And, in the thirteen years since I've been back in New Zealand, I've searched the country for the place where I could have that sense of belonging and place again. I've lived in Queenstown, Arrowtown, Glenorchy (three times), Dunedin, Wellington (three times), Napier, Mount Maunganui and now – Laingholm, Auckland.

I search and I search and I search, all the while knowing that what I am looking for can never be found externally.

Or can it?

Where does the spiritual path leave off and the real world come in? How do they intertwine and meet each other? Because we humans are tribal beings; we crave connection, and belonging, and being seen as worthy. We want to feel like we have something to offer our community that is needed and valued.

And when we grow up in a family that doesn't embed within us a sense of being connected, a sense of belonging, and a sense of being seen as worthy, it's possible that we're doomed to never know how to create those things externally. How can that which is not felt within ever be experienced without?

Because while I felt connected in Whistler, while I felt like I belonged, while I felt like I was part of a community... I still wasn't completely at home within myself. I needed the drugs to access that place. The weed and the booze and the ecstasy and the blow and the mushrooms and the acid.

After the psychosis, and the psych ward, and the broken engagement, and the hasty trip back to New Zealand... I heard from very few people in my community. One phone call, from one friend. That's all I remember. Granted, this was in the days before social media and free calling via the Internet and phone apps. But there were still the possibilities of emails and letters and international calls on calling cards. I received one call, from one person, from that town I was sure was home.

I felt like I'd been ejected, forgotten, spat out and pasted over.

- *Who was that girl again? What happened to her?*
- *Oh her, yeah she took too many drugs and ended up going crazy. She's in a mental hospital, somewhere.*
- *Too bad. She was hot. Great dancer.*
- *Totally.*

Meanwhile, I was living at my Mum's, sleeping until 2pm every day, dragging myself out of bed, and forcing myself to do yoga because I knew it could help. It wasn't even the town where I'd grown up – Dunedin – as Mum had only recently taken the job at Glenorchy School. I knew no one in that town, and I didn't care to know anyone either. Glenorchy seemed to mainly consist of farmers, drop outs and uncool people who had never travelled, didn't know what yoga was, and certainly hadn't opened any doors of perception with mind-expanding offerings like mushrooms and acid like I had.

Oh yes, I took all my unworthy feelings and projected them on to the people around me. And as soon as I could get the money together for a flight, I bought a one-way ticket to Auckland. I didn't give myself any time to heal and recover. Nope. Within four weeks or so I was heading to the Big Smoke to seek my fame and fortune as a journalist

18

and prove that I was no crazy woman. That I wasn't a failure. That I was worth something.

It was barely November 2004, only a few months after my release from Lion's Gate Hospital.

I found a flat with a friend's sister and her boyfriend. I dropped back into the circle of friends I had known in Auckland when I'd lived there during Uni days almost a decade earlier. But I didn't feel like I belonged, and I couldn't relate to anybody. No one seemed to have the same creative buzz and energy of my Whistler Tribe, and even landing a waitressing job at a swanky new waterfront bar and restaurant failed to make me feel any better.

In fact, it made me feel worse. I'd quit waitressing the year before to pursue my writing career full-time, even seen some minor success with a screenplay. Now here I was, almost 30, serving people food and booze again.

Then there was the constant sensory overload.

Because that psychosis… it wasn't just psychosis. It couldn't just be psychosis. I couldn't just be crazy. It felt like something more – it felt like some kind of awakening. And the awakening aspect of my experience had blasted open all my sensory receptors. The city, with its overloaded psychic airwaves, overwhelmed me. Driving was a nightmare – the lights and the cars and the sounds and the traffic. The supermarket pummelled me – I felt like I was in a Stephen King novel and everyone else was a zombie. Nothing was as it had been. Reality wasn't how I remembered it. And when I was turned down as the editor of *Sky Magazine* while on a weekend trip to Raglan, my fake-it-til-you-make-it confidence crumbled. I started sobbing on the drive back to Auckland when I hit the Bombay Hills and I just couldn't stop.

I cried all the way to the North Shore. I cried all that night. I woke up crying. I did make it out of bed, and into a heap at the foot of the bed, but still crying. Finally, I managed to call my younger sister, crying. Somehow, I was able to be vulnerable in front of her. She'd lived in Whistler with me for a short time. She'd partied with me, and opened up conversations about our childhood. And she'd started doing personal work. My sister understood more than anyone else in our family.

19

She got me.

"You need support. You need to heal. You've got to give yourself time. Why don't you go and stay at Nana and Pop's? I'm sure they'll have you?"

Nana and Pop.

My Dad's parents.

They'd always lived in the same town as us when we were kids, moving from Dunedin to Oamaru when we did, and from Oamaru to Blenheim with my Dad after he'd divorced my Mum and married Viv.

They were the one consistent, unchanging, steady, and always-to-be-depended on part of my childhood. Yes! I could go there. I could get in my new $800 car, bought with borrowed money after I cajoled an old lover into taking me to Ellerslie Car Fair one Sunday, and I could drive to Blenheim.

And so I did.

I called my manager at the swanky new waterside restaurant – still crying – and resigned. I confronted my flatmates – still crying – and told them I had to leave. Then I drove eight hours straight to Wellington, jumped on the 2am ferry, and arrived at my Nana and Pop's brick and tile house with it's immaculately manicured lawn and gardens at 6am. Shattered, I left everything in the car, including a peace lily potted plant, and gratefully let Nana lead me into the guest room where I was to stay. There, I fell asleep until night.

Safe, at last.

I'd made it.

Although the peace lily didn't. It was a hot early December day, and the car interior was at desert temperatures. By the time I went out to unpack the next day, the peace lily had wilted into oblivion, and nothing I did could revive it.

* * *

Laingholm, 2017

The spider plant now on my altar drove with my son and I all the way from Glenorchy in a plastic bag. It took Sam and I a week to drive up both islands, staying with friends and family along the way, and the spider plant ended up staying in that plastic bag for four weeks. No water. Just a cutting from the plant I'd owned in Queenstown back in 2004.

It wasn't until we got here, to this house, our second house in two weeks in Auckland, that I finally found an old jam jar to sit the cutting in.

Three weeks without water it lasted.

Two weeks in water, no soil, before I finally planted it.

Now, three days after I planted it, I swear it has doubled in size.

Resilient, those spider plants. Resilient.

Follow the Light

S hafts of morning sunlight slice across the room and edge up onto the couch. They seduce me down on to the floor where I can soak up more of their warmth.

Sun has been rare since we moved to Auckland a month ago.

From my low vantage point, I watch a spider's web strung between the decking's edge flash bright in the breeze as the sun catches it. The light glints off the lights strung along the deck. Everywhere I look, there's sunlight bouncing, reflecting, and flashing.

I sit here for almost two hours. Holding space on the phone while my lover/ex-lover goes through a deep emotional process and unlocks a trauma that has dictated decades of self-destructive behaviour. I watch the light dance as he dives into the darkness.

He's the first long-term partner I've had since leaving my son's father seven years ago. But he lives in Europe, and we're attempting to skilfully navigate a long-distance relationship focused on healing and waking up.

Or at least we were. Which is why I say lover/ex-lover. We were lovers until May this year, 2017, when he chose to sleep with someone else and I chose to break up with him. Now, in September, we're considering coming back together. Or we are back together but haven't seen each other in the flesh to confirm whether that's the right choice. Which means we're on the phone for a couple of hours every day, often doing this kind of deep emotional work. Holding each other, from 12,000 miles away.

He knows this work well, as he does it for a living, and he only needs me to be there. Not saying anything, just being there, holding him. So I sit, feeling the urge to check my phone arise, choosing not to respond, knowing that the moment my attention is engaged elsewhere, I'm no longer present with him, and I'm no longer holding space.

Instead, I feel the sun on my skin and watch it dance across the surfaces that catch my eyes.

The moment stretches and opens and welcomes me in.

There is nothing to do. Nowhere to go. This is it. This is all there is.

Ah... contentment. So much deeper than happiness, so much more potent, so much more real. Contentment leads me into the perfection of this moment as it is, and I am grateful for it this morning.

This is why I do the work.

This is why I turned away from chasing the external markings of success.

This is aliveness.

* * *

Off the phone, space holding complete, I flash back to another morning, another sun, another September.

Whistler, 2004

It was the Sunday morning before I ended up in the psych ward the second time.

I was in my home office lying on the carpet and feeling the late summer's warmth permeating my skin. Madonna's *American Life* album was on repeat. Over and over again it played as I stared up through the slats of the wooden blinds at the sun blazing through the window.

Was I alive then? Or had I checked out completely?

It was only four days since my fiancé had broken up with me and moved out of the three-bedroom town house we shared with one other flatmate.

Then, lying on the floor in the sun staring out the window...

That wasn't contentment.

That was the freeze response.

Twenty-four hours later, the cops would pick me up on the back roads of Pemberton, about 45 minutes North of Whistler, after they were called in by a logging truck driver. I'd leapt up on the back of his truck and raced across the stacked logs, yanking off marker tags. In my deluded mind, these logging tags were contest flags from the then-popular TV show *Fear Factor*. The more flags I tore off, the more successful I would be. The more chance I would win. And I was determined to win. So determined, that I almost leapt from the logs to the truck cabin… at a height of maybe 15 feet or so. I was running. I was in flow. I was on *Fear Factor*. I was going to win. I was going to leap. But I didn't. Survival instinct I guess – even in the midst of the craziness. I knew I wouldn't make it.

Instead, I scuttled down the side of the logs, yanked open the passenger door and rolled into the cab where the driver was still sitting. He tried to grab me, but I rolled into the back, behind the front seats, where he had a mattress and duvet, and out the other side, avoiding him and running off back down the road, barefoot, to retrieve my hoodie.

That's why he'd called the cops – to let them know about the crazy woman leaping onto his moving truck and racing down the top before rolling in and out of the cab.

Oh, and I was also topless. Even crazier.

But you know – *Fear Factor*! In my mind I was a contestant and it was all being filmed. Leaping onto a moving logging truck was way more impressive if done topless.

And I never do anything topless.

I don't even lie topless on the beach. Not even on the topless beach.

So what the hell was I doing? It was craziness. Insanity!

Right?

Well… yes and no. To the casual observer – the truck driver, the two cops that found me skipping stones into a mountain stream awhile later, the medical staff at Pemberton Clinic where they took me – it appeared that I was crazy. Nothing I was saying or doing made any sense in their world.

From my perspective though, everything made total sense. I was taking the external circumstances unfolding around me and using them to prop up a fantasy that my mind was conjuring to protect me from emotional pain.

Skilful huh?

My actions were the logical and sustained result of a defence mechanism, in overdrive, pouring everything it could into avoiding emotional pain.

In my mind, my actions all made total sense.

Because, that was how I had lived for 29 years. I was ninja-skilled at avoiding any emotional pain through a combination of reframing and suppressing. And the thing about avoiding emotional pain is there comes a point when no matter how fucking strong your defences are, you just can't hold back the dam anymore. My defences were strong enough, and did their job so well, that they pushed me all the way over into apparent insanity.

That is, my reframed constructs of reality shifted more and more away from consensus reality. For example, a car with Ontario plates parked outside of our housing complex was proof that my fiancé's Ontario-based family was beginning to gather for our secret wedding.

Small things – seen, experienced, and perceived in a way that would keep me safe from the intense emotional pain I just couldn't face.

Five nights earlier, my fiancé had broken up with me and moved out of our shared home. That's what had precipitated this second episode of psychosis, exactly one month after the first. Unable to face the grief, the heartache and the agony of him leaving... and unable to face the consequences of the relationship break-up... my mind went into protection overdrive.

What was really fascinating though, is that there was another part of me observing all of this occurring. That part of me knew something wasn't right – it wasn't strong enough to reach out and change anything. All she could do was watch as my conditioned mind and my defence mechanisms spun further and further out of control.

And that was terrifying.

* * *

Who is She that watches? Who is the witness? The observer?

It's the first step in a meditation practice – learning to sit back and watch the thoughts rather than identify with the thoughts. The first step in beginning to learn who we truly are, and what we truly are not.

I'd become adept at this process, not through a formal meditation practice, but via a post-waitressing wind-down practice I'd adopted in 2000.

Little did I know that this practice would one day both lead to psychosis *and* allow me to understand and recover from psychosis. Back then, it just felt like the right thing to do.

I would come home at 2am from an eight-hour waitressing shift wired as all hell and desperate to sleep. My method? Smoke a tiny bit of weed in my pipe (an eighth would last me three months) – slip into bed with my mini-disc player and do savasana while listening to music.

What ensued was an altered state of reality where I would drop down underneath my thoughts and observe them as if flying over a landscape that shifted and morphed according to the beats and rhythms of the music.

Not just any music either – trance music.

The name says it all.

Trance music and marijuana. These days I know marijuana as a sacred plant medicine capable of opening the doors to other realms of existence. Back then, like most people, I thought it was just a fun, recreational drug that helped me chill out after working all night.

But marijuana is powerful.

And meditation is powerful.

To the untrained and unaware initiate, combining these powerful practices and plant guides with no understanding of the terrain about to be traversed… is dangerous as all hell.

Add in a life-long psychological pattern of repressing and suppressing emotional pain – a pattern of denying truth and shutting or at least reframing, reality – and you have all the ingredients required for psychosis.

And, as it turned out, for an awakening.

Because somehow, for unknown reasons, at age 29, although I was psychologically well defended and had little self-awareness, I was also ripe to wake up. My consciousness was ready to evolve.

That August and September of 2004, this explosive mix of circumstances whirled ever tighter in and around me. My relationship put the squeeze on my emotional and mental holding patterns, forcing me into deeper and darker corners with every passing month. My increasing dedication to yoga and meditation activated and opened up channels of energy in my body. And my use of drugs – particularly mushrooms, marijuana and acid – turbo-charged everything.

There was no escape.

It could only have ever gone one way.

* * *

Laingholm, 2017

I'm listening to Madonna's *American Life* now, writing this. I don't particularly like the album. I only bought it out of loyalty for Madonna – I was still buying every Madonna album back in 2004. Despite not liking it, that morning in Whistler, five days after my fiancé had left me, the album held me entranced for hours. It held me while I did what I did best – float away, disassociate, convince myself that I was okay, that my fiancé dumping me was all working out for the best, that nothing could touch me, that nothing could hurt me.

This is true, on a particular spiritual level, but this particular spiritual truth is also eminently co-optable by those who easily disassociate. That is – combine an intellectual understanding of spirituality with a pattern of disassociation, and you have a recipe for spiritual bypassing: the act of ignoring the real pain of being human in favour of spiritual bliss and ecstasy.

That's where I was at that morning in Whistler, lying on the floor as the music held me in the sun's warm caress. I didn't cry, I didn't grieve, and I didn't feel anything.

I was bypassing my humanness.

That's not life.

Nor is it aliveness.

But it was me, back then, doing what I'd always done and trying really fucking hard to survive the only way I knew how. That's what my crazy was – maybe what all crazy is. It's just our conditioned mind, our defences, attempting to keep us safe the only way we know how. We take what is happening and we filter it through our mind to create a version of reality that feels safe. Because safety is the original survival instinct – it's hard-wired into us. For some, our emotional landscapes are so intense and painful that our survival instinct isn't just applied to our physical reality, but also to our emotional reality. Just as our body would do everything it could to avoid a lion on the savannah, so too was my emotional and mental self doing everything it could to avoid the reality of the break-up with my fiancé.

And when I was in the Pemberton medical clinic, after they'd given me sedatives, before the ambulance showed up to drive me two hours down the road to Lion's Gate Acute Psych Ward again, I knew something was wrong.

That deeper part of me – the witness – knew something was wrong.

But I didn't know how to bring myself back. I didn't know how to calm myself down. I didn't know how to reassure myself that I was safe and that it was okay to turn off all the internal defence mechanisms. That it was okay to grieve and cry and feel the pain of betrayal and heartache.

I didn't know what to do, and that was terrifying too.

* * *

Whistler, 2004

There was a sink in the small room they'd put me in, after the cops took me to the Pemberton Medial Clinic. It was part of the bench that housed the rubbish bin, along the same wall as the door, which was open, but guarded. Two RCMP cops flanked each side of the door, chatting away. One of them had just moved from Ontario and his wife was finding it hard to adjust. Throughout the small talk, I could feel them keeping one eye on the crazy woman. What was she going to do next?

Someone brought me a filled roll – I'd begged for food when they'd put me in the room. I hadn't eaten in at least a day and knew that my body needed food. Apparently, it wasn't in the Clinic's policy to give patients food, but I persisted long enough that they'd relented and turned up with this filled roll, wrapped in thin plastic – Glad Wrap, as we call it here in New Zealand.

A filled roll made of – soggy white bread – with meat in it. I recoiled. I couldn't eat that kind of food – there was no prana in that food. No aliveness. And so I picked out the lettuce and the tomatoes and ate them before tossing the rest in the bin. I was acutely aware that these actions looked like the actions of a crazy woman, but I was unable to explain – to verbalise – why I had begged for food only to throw it away.

I could feel them, looking at me, seeing Crazy, and I knew that everything I did confirmed what they had already decided. And I was petrified of this – of them only seeing crazy. Yet I had to do what I had to do. I couldn't eat meat and white bread, so in the bin it went.

And next, what I had to do was run my wrists under the tap.

It felt like this was necessary. Even though it seemed crazy. But somehow it felt like the cold running water would help to ground me, and that it would help bring me back into my self and back down from this place I seemed to have become lost in.

It didn't work though.

Nor did the yoga I tried to do.

Nothing worked.

Nothing but the sedatives they gave me.

The last thing I remember from the Pemberton Medical Clinic is being loaded into the back of the ambulance on a stretcher, possibly strapped down. Then I was out.

And when I woke up, I was sane again. Sane, but committed to a psych ward and unable to leave by choice until they decided that I was no longer a risk to society.

But thanks to my fiancé dumping me, I was now single, potentially homeless and broke. So yeah, that too. Not that being broke was his fault – I was the one who had quit a well-paying waitressing gig to pursue her dreams of being a screenwriter and creating a local TV show. It didn't matter whose fault it was though.

I'd woken up and found myself lost.

The Emotional Guidance System

Laingholm, 2017

Gratitude, this morning, for the skills I've developed in navigating my internal world, and my emotional landscape, over the last 14 years.

Hands press together in prayer, thumbs touching my heart centre, slight bow of the head. Mantra plays through my headphones as I sit on my sheepskin rug, leaning against a yoga bolster, balancing my laptop on my lap.

All is well in this moment.

All was not well half an hour ago, three hours ago, twelve hours ago.

The medical establishment might describe my experience as mood swings, a symptom of bipolar disorder. It implies a haphazard, randomly fluctuating swing of emotional states of being.

This medical description however, is not my lived experience.

My lived experience, hard won, is that there is always a reason as to why I'm feeling what I'm feeling. My lived experience is that if I can allow myself to deeply feel the emotion, and listen to the wisdom it brings that I can use this wisdom to navigate my life in an increasingly skilled manner.

Welcome to the emotional guidance system. It's something that my childhood defense mechanisms shut me off from completely. Instead, unknown to me, I was mostly navigating my life unconsciously through the strongest emotion I wasn't able to feel, because I was unaware of how constant it was in my life.

Fear.

That decision I made in 1995 to stay in Auckland and transfer to Auckland University after a three-month holiday, during which time my first love broke up with me long-distance from our hometown of Dunedin? Fear-based. I was afraid of going back to Dunedin and having to confront how I felt about the end of that relationship, afraid of bumping into my ex with his new girlfriend, afraid of facing our joint friends. Afraid.

The decision, in 1996, to head overseas and join my next boyfriend on his big OE (overseas experience) in London the day after I graduated from my journalism course? Fear-based. I was afraid to apply for jobs as a journalist, afraid to get posted to a hick town in the middle of nowhere, afraid of the old boys' network and the rampant-yet-denied sexism of the industry.

The decision to go on holiday to Costa Rica in May 2004 with my fiancé even though I was falling into deeper and deeper debt on my meagre writing income? Fear-based. I was afraid that if he went without me he would cheat on me, for sure. I was afraid that it would be the end of the relationship. I was afraid of missing out.

I

was

afraid.

And I didn't even know it.

* * *

When you have no relationship with your emotional experience, it will guide you unconsciously. And it will be the hard-wired instinct for safety and security that pushes you forward through life.

Fear-based living. The way most people live. It's the reason why we experience a fucked-up world in so many ways. We're afraid of what other people think of us. We're afraid of leaving the job that's destroying us. We're afraid of ending the relationship that's sucking us dry. We're afraid of chasing our dreams. We're afraid. All. The. Time.

Last night, on the phone to my lover/ex-lover in Croatia, I was deep in an emotional abyss. I felt vulnerable, afraid, and full of tears.

Tears that had been tugging at my awareness all day, resurfacing when I stopped to do a ten-minute yoga practice in the kitchen. And then, with nothing but my breath, awareness and body playing out through the movement and postures, the tears broke through and the sobs came.

There was no ignoring them any longer. I had to go in and see what was going on. Why the emotion? Yet the resistance was strong – it's challenging to persuade the mind/body to feel pain when it can choose not to. I knew I could get on my mat and that would take me there, as it has hundreds of times in the last 15 years. But I couldn't make myself. Doing a stop, drop and yoga practice in the kitchen had been challenging enough. The idea of changing out of jeans into yoga pants and rolling out a mat seemed impossible.

Instead, I called my ex-lover/lover. I asked him to take me through a process. To hold me in love while asking me how I'm feeling, and then, how that makes me feel, and how that makes me feel, and how that makes me feel. When he does this process, there's no escaping, because his intuitive and tuned-in self can often feel what I'm feeling before I can. I can't hide from him the way I can hide from myself, plus I can feel his love and care and concern for me. Then it's not so scary to feel the intense emotions.

But he couldn't do it. He couldn't drop in and hold me, nor verbally guide me.

He had too much going on himself.

And when he couldn't do it, and I was already sobbing my heart out and needed so badly to be held, to be witnessed, to be loved and seen... and he couldn't do it... that triggered another layer of doubt about our relationship, which I had ended three months ago. And was now considering restarting.

My emotion plus the doubts. Multiplied by the doubts. Childhood trauma squared with insecurity over current life circumstances. Emotion compounded. Relationship questioned. Who can hold me now?

I got off the phone adrift, and watched as I sat comatose on the bed, arms crossed, studying the emotion, stopping the flow, shutting down.

This is happening, and while it's happening, I'm witnessing it happening.

I'm aware of myself – aware of being stuck and refusing to feel. I'm afraid, and I'm giving in to the fear. I'm going into freeze, which leads to disassociation.

Eventually, I allow myself to lie down and the tears erupt again while a single sentence plays over and over in my head as I sob myself to sleep.

"I want to go home. I want to go home. I want to go home."

* * *

And I do. I do want to go home, more than anything else in my life right now except for my desire to be in a deeply intimate relationship with a man. I want to be home and I want to be home with Him.

Yet my ex-lover/lover, my man, Him... he lives in Croatia, an hour from his young son. Unable to leave to be with me. And I am here, with my young son, in New Zealand, unwilling to go there because I know my place is in this country, for now.

Stuck.

Between this connection we have and my desire to be at home with my man – emotional terror compounded.

He and I have been navigating this territory since May 2016, when we came together in New Zealand after leading retreat together. That retreat led to a retreat business, which brought us together in Bali, Mexico, Croatia (twice) and New Zealand (twice).

We broke up in June 2017.

Then we led a retreat together in Mexico in July 2017.

We explored coming back together in September of that year. And now he's coming to New Zealand again, on November 1st, 2017 for six weeks. We've got two retreats booked in that time and intend to see if the personal work we've both done since May means we can now come together.

Turns out we're both deathly afraid of emotional intimacy and have all kinds of subtle and secretive defence systems that dance around deceiving us that they're keeping us safe while actually denying us the very thing we crave.

Mood swings?

Bipolar disorder?

Crazy?

Ha!

It's just life – and me, navigating the challenges of life, which trigger childhood trauma, and creating out-of-context reactions.

As the childhood trauma is cleared, the challenges become easier to navigate, which reveals new and deeper layers of trauma. And whether we realise it consciously or not, most of us experienced a lot of trauma as a child. Not necessarily the big, standout moments of trauma like physical or sexual abuse, but the insidious on-going trauma of emotional neglect – of not been seen or validated in childhood for who we are. In my generation, and earlier, most of us learned pretty damn fast as children that we need to act in certain ways in order to be loved – that there are parts of us that are not acceptable and must be hidden away. Especially if we have authoritarian parents. Or parents with no emotional literacy. Or both.

I learned that emotions were not acceptable and that my emotional self had to be hidden away. And I became so good at hiding my emotional self away that I lost the ability to feel her at all.

* * *

Laingholm, 2017

Last night, getting off the phone to my ex-lover, I curled into a ball, sobbing myself to sleep, heart aching for home, remembering… I was 29, coming back to New Zealand to a home that wasn't. I was 22, living in Chamonix with nine people in a three-bedroom house, triggered as all hell and unconscious of what was happening. I was 12 again, moving to Dunedin after my parents divorced, to a house that never became a home. I was a baby, alone in a cot, desperate to be held and to be loved.

The body remembers it all – everything that was never fully felt at the time. The body stores it, waiting for a time when it can be safely felt, acknowledged and released, once and for all. But if we don't know that that's what's happening, our lives can become this increasingly volatile, unstable, overwhelming emotional minefield where nothing ever feels right and we're always struggling to hold it together.

Me, I have no problem falling apart anymore. I know that I need to fall apart in order to become whole again. I need to un-do myself in order to remake myself into a woman capable of living a fulfilling life of connection and service.

And what I need is a home.

A place where I feel safe, secure and loved. A place where I can create and express myself. A place where I can connect and engage with people who love and value me. A place where I can be.

* * *

It's the great Kiwi dream – to own your own home. Everybody used to do it, once upon a time. It was just a given. Go to school, go to Uni, get a job, buy a house, get married, and settle down.

As a teenager, all I wanted to do was travel the world and have adventures. All I wanted to do was get the hell out of home. But home wasn't home, and I didn't know it. I didn't know that I was deeply craving something that had long been denied to me, likely since I was about 7 or 8 when everything began to fall apart in our family.

Now, I feel it. I feel that which I couldn't feel for almost forty years and it's intense and, at times, overwhelming. Now, I see all the decisions I made – or didn't make – because, unconsciously, I was craving a home. And these unconscious decisions have snowballed into all kinds of messes.

This is what it means to live unconsciously. This is what it means to be asleep, to be mired in Maya – illusion. Most of us live from this space, whether we realise it or not.

* * *

Whistler, 2004

I was completely unconscious of what was driving my behaviour until I was 29 years old. I thought it was one thing – Fuck yeah! I'm heading overseas for big adventure! – when often, it was the exact

36

opposite – Fuck no! I can't cope with entering the world of journalism as a young, insecure woman with poor boundaries. Get me the hell out of here!

Then I woke up.

That was the first psychosis.

AKA awakening.

Even the psychiatrist I saw at Lion's Gate Acute Psych Ward agreed. "Spiritual burglary," he called it, while also adding "bipolar disorder" to my notes and writing out a prescription.

Likely it was the strange prostrations to the Sun God Ra that I was doing in his office, on my knees, in all four directions, that gave it away.

Or maybe the strange foreign language I was speaking when my fiancé drove me down to the hospital. He reckoned it was ancient Egyptian, which fit nicely with the 'knowing' I was experiencing that my fiancé and I had been together in a past life in Egypt. We'd been lovers, and I had betrayed him. And now, in this lifetime, I had to pay that karma back while loving him unconditionally, even though I knew inside that he was going to break up with me within the month.

Crazed delusion?

Or truth?

Because he did break-up with me within the month, just as I knew he would.

He sat me down on the couch on a Tuesday night, laid it out, and then left the house. I wandered around in a daze, fell asleep, and woke up with a brand new mole on the side of my face the size of a dime.

I'd just finished reading an article about how moles and freckles often reflect past life experiences.

The mole lasted three days – long enough for my girlfriend to witness it, freak out, and demand I see a doctor. But before I could make an appointment, it had scabbed up and fallen off. As if something deep and painful and dark had been forced out of my internal world, through my skin and released forever.

Karma.

Paid.

That break-up had yet to unfold, as I sun-prostrated myself in the psychiatrist's office at Lions Gate, but I knew it was coming. Just as I already knew my fiancé would end up in a relationship with my girlfriend – the same one freaked out by the mole. I knew that too. And possibly it was that knowing which had tipped my awakening over into psychosis. Because it's one thing to feel the Universe wrap you in her warm embrace and whisper all her secrets as you sink into the bliss of Oneness.

It's another when one of those secrets is that your fiancé and your best friend are going to be together.

The Safety of Grandparents

Laingholm, 2017

I wake up the next morning, after those sobs of home-yearning, and stare out at the Waitakere Ranges that border our house. My heart still aches – yes, I want a home, but does such a place even exist?

I had a home once – 42 Arun Street, Oamaru – with a big wattle tree in the front garden and a fishpond outside the front door where I would sit with a row of rocks collected from the driveway. That and a paintbrush. I would dip my brush in the fishpond and paint a rock wet, placing it down on the other side of me, before picking up the next rock and painting it wet. Down the row I would go, and by the time I'd painted the last rock wet, the first rock was dry and ready to go again.

There were plans to extend the house – to create another bedroom, or an extra lounge. I don't remember now. I do remember the fishpond would have gone. But before that happened, my parents split up and that was the end of home. My Dad moved out, the house went on the market, and we three kids moved with Mum down to Dunedin. I was 12. My childhood was over.

Except… there was another place that continued to hold the energy of home.

Nana and Pop's house. My Dad's parents.

No matter where they lived – Dunedin, Oamaru, Blenheim and then finally Thames – their place felt like home. That was why, when I found myself dissolving into eternal tears in Auckland in 2004, I fled down the country to Nana and Pop's house, the closest thing to home I knew.

And as I recuperated that December of 2004 at my Nana and Pop's, all the tiny details of the past few months cycled through my head. Each day I would wake at first light and lie motionless in the spare room, staring at the wallpaper and the ceiling, recalling every tiny detail of both episodes of psychosis.

When had each episode begun? What had triggered them? What had unfolded? What was delusion and what was truth? Surely it hadn't just been mental illness? Something else was going on…

As my mind played the loops over and over, I observed my body in this moment, pyjama-clad and still, tucked under the duvet in my grandparents' spare room. Strange sensations filled my belly and my chest every morning – waves and bubbles of varying intensity. There seemed to be no physical reason for these sensations and I'd never experienced anything like them before.

Invariably, at just after 8am, my Pop would rap on my door as he walked down the hallway. "Morning," he'd say.

And that was it.

But it was enough.

Without that rap, without that word, I might have been able to rationalise and justify staying in bed until mid-morning or later. But I couldn't disappoint my Pop.

Up I would get, pulling on clothes so I could go sit at the same ornate, circular dining table I remembered from my childhood. Twenty years on, it was still covered with a round embroidered velvet cloth that in turn would be covered by a square cotton tablecloth for meals.

The table was laid just so, every night, for nigh on fifty years or more I imagine. I never knew a night – or a morning – at my Nana and Pop's house when the table wasn't laid the night before, nor the porridge not already on the stove, soaking, ready to be made the next morning.

We would sit and eat that porridge, with toast in a toast holder and Craig's jam in a little dish, cups of tea to wash it all down, and talk about everything except what had happened to me and why I was there.

Then we would come together again at morning tea, this time in the conservatory where the morning sun poured in, onto a jigsaw puzzle set up on the folding plastic table, covered with a piece of plywood to create a bigger surface. Nana and Pop would share stories from their youth – of the nightman who would come round in the night (hence his name) – to collect the buckets of sewerage from all the houses. They would speak of bringing up five children after the war, of Nana hiding under the bed when it all got too much. I would listen, mentally taking note of details, aware that this could be the last time I heard this story, or this story, or this story.

And then there was lunch, again at the round table in the dining room. Afternoon tea in the lounge followed by tea in the dining room, never later than 6pm, because the news began at 6pm and had to be watched in the lounge.

My grandparents, and the routine, and the furniture, and the stories and even the paintings on the wall were all the same as they had been. The order of their existence provided the container my chaos needed to begin the healing process. There was nowhere to run anymore. I finally had to stop and face what had happened to me.

And that meant admitting that proper employment wasn't an option right now. So if I wanted to pay board to my grandparents – which I most definitely did – then I had to go and apply for a Sickness Benefit. Which meant I had to go and see a doctor and get a medical certificate to officially declare my unwellness.

I don't remember seeing the doctor, but I do remember the Work and Income Office. Mostly, I remember how fragile, shaky and vulnerable I felt. Like shards of eggshell ready to splinter into a hundred different directions. My arrival coincided with the departure of a very angry man waving his arms around and yelling at the top of his voice. He was being ushered out as I walked through the doors.

My stomach dropped as his hostility pierced through every layer of my being and tears sprang into my eyes.

How on earth was I going to do this? I almost turned around and fled, but a manager – a man in his mid-40s – had clocked me and he came and steered me towards a seat and sat me down. With the utmost care and kindness, he took me through all the paperwork necessary to ensure that I had some money coming in every week. Money given to me because I was now termed mentally ill.

41

"You'll be on those pills for life, that's it for you now," a well-meaning family member had admonished me. Unable to respond, retort or refute her pronouncement, I knew it wouldn't be so.

I always knew it wouldn't be so.

But that month at my grandparents, I was too weak, too vulnerable and too fragile to do anything about it yet. I took my diagnosis and used it to get the money I needed to support my healing. And I kept taking the pills I'd been prescribed.

And I watched, fascinated, every morning, the varying sensations in my belly and heart space. I watched, and tracked and correlated, and began to notice that the intensity of those morning sensations was directly related to the intensity of the sobbing that would always come later in the day.

Intense morning sensations equalled buckets of tears being vomited out – mostly in the shower, because I prayed that the sound would cover my wails and not disturb my grandparents. Tears also found me on the runs I forced myself to take every day in an attempt to get some positive endorphins flowing in my system. Anything to feel better. Anything to hide from my grandparents the waves of emotion that rolled through me.

Mild morning sensations equalled moderate tears and sobs.

I began to dread the sensations, even as I realised that there was body wisdom at play here. Because surely – surely! – all these tears couldn't be because of what had happened?

Maybe the first week. Or the first three weeks. But the tears went on, and on, and on. I cried every day I was at my grandparents, sometimes for hours on end – in the shower, in child's pose, on my run, silently into the pillow. I continued the crying when I left there and headed back to Glenorchy for the safety of my mother's now-empty house. She'd gone to Australia for four weeks, and I discovered that without her there, Glenorchy was bearable. It wasn't so much the place after all, but the close proximity of my loving and caring mother that made me want to run.

I cried every day when I moved into a three-bedroom house in Queenstown, in early 2005, with two other girlfriends who had come from Whistler. All of us refugees from the party lifestyle, all of us broken and healing in our own way.

For four months or so, every single day, I cried. And cried. And cried some more. And then it happened.

It finally happened.

There was a day – an entire day – when I did not cry.

Not a single tear.

And that day, when it finally came and passed, signalled that this too would pass. That I would somehow live through the implosion of my life and the explosion of my mind and the shattering of my dreams and self-image, and that I too would rise from the ashes of it all, like the Egyptian bennu.

But it was painful. Excruciatingly painful. I wanted my life back. I wanted my fiancé back. Or at least, I wanted back the love we'd shared when the love was great. And I wanted ME back.

I did not want to be where I was, and I did not want to be who I was.

My understanding of yoga had not yet deepened enough, nor was my self-awareness strong enough, to stop me from creating extra layers of suffering because of this intense resistance to my circumstances. I hated what had happened, and I hated where I was, and I hated who I had become.

Yet even with all that resistance I also persisted in dragging myself up and through every single day.

I moved – walking and running on a daily basis.

I stayed away from alcohol – completely for four months, and then mostly in moderation. The one or two occasions when I indulged like my former party girl self, I crumpled in on myself in all directions, and became someone I hated even more.

I wrote – journaling through my experience to make sense of everything that had occurred.

I practised – mostly yoga, because given the awakening experiences I'd had, meditation seemed a dangerous thing. I was cautious of anything that might trigger the intense flows of Kundalini that I knew had triggered many of my symptoms.

Ah Kundalini... Kundalini... the evolution of consciousness in action. That which allows us to cut through the mind and simply know the deepest truths. That which is both creative energy and the energy of self-expression. Kundalini is wisdom, transformation and the power of infinite consciousness within. In other words, when Kundalini awakens... some serious shit starts to go down because our whole perception of reality and Self shifts and changes.

Shit that can look exactly like mental illness – sometimes referred to as the Kali stage of awakening. So-named because Kali is the most ferocious of the Hindu Goddesses.

Because I knew – I had always known – that my experiences were not just mania. I wasn't bipolar disorder. In fact, when I finally started researching "bipolar disorder", it struck me that maybe nobody was bipolar. That in fact being bipolar disorder was simply a way of labelling a collection of symptoms that doctors didn't really understand, that had certain impacts on people's lives.

Fourteen years on, that's my perspective and I'm holding to it. People are not necessarily 'mentally ill'. People exhibit a collection of behaviours, which are symptoms of the Mind's determination to avoid uncomfortable feelings, stay safe, and meet unconscious needs. And, which are often an indication that the psyche is ready to evolve and heal those patterns.

In certain people, those behaviours show up in a pattern our Western Medical Model calls "bipolar disorder".

But it's not a disease. You can't test for it. And – if my experience can prove anything – once you get comfortable with uncomfortable feelings, identify and meet your unconscious needs, and heal the root traumas from childhood, and beyond...

Those behaviours don't show up anymore.

* * *

Queenstown 2005

One morning, I did make an appointment with the local mental health services, because the Canadians had recommended I do this when I got back to New Zealand. To 'get support'.

44

It was shortly after I'd moved to Queenstown, maybe February 2005. Almost six months since I'd been diagnosed. The nurse who greeted me was patronising and saw me solely through the definition of my label. There was no recognition or connection with me as a person.

None of this was blatant, or deliberate on her part. She was just doing her job. However, the awakening experience had left me with an ability to perceive and read the subtlest of signals from people – a gift of insight that would serve me well later on when I began teaching yoga and leading retreats.

But in that moment, in that meeting, I knew that being in the mental health system was not going to be helpful for my recovery. That I needed to step outside the belief system and ideas of the Western Medical Model and pursue my own way of finding context and meaning for what had happened to me. I knew THAT was the key that would enable me to live a well and powerful life.

So I never went back.

And, two months after I had moved into 'The Lily Pad', as us three Whistler refugees affectionately called our flat on Queenstown Hill, I announced to my girlfriends that I was cutting down on my prescriptions.

"I'm halving my dosage, and once that stabilises and all seems well, I'm halving it again. And again. And again, until I'm off. I need you to keep an eye on me and let me know straight away if my behaviour is becoming at all erratic."

My mum already knew of my plans and had agreed to give me feedback too. And that felt safe – that my trusted friends who I lived with, and my Mum, were all keeping an eye on me. Because I knew that I needed to get off the drugs, and get off them now, but I also wanted to be responsible about it.

Ange, my Aussie girlfriend, had gone through a similar experience to mine in Whistler. Only she had been living in a cabin by herself in the woods at the time and was able to ground her experience and contain her spiralling mind in such a way that she never drew attention to herself. (No jumping onto the back of logging trucks for her!) So she understood what I had gone through, and the kind of support I needed.

Juanita, a fellow Kiwi I'd met in Chamonix over a pool table, also had her own experiences to draw on.

But it was still a test for me. What if I was mistaken and deluded and there was something wrong with me? What if I went into mania again?

My relentless examination of the days, weeks and months leading up to the psychosis had convinced me that both incidents were related, and yet slightly different. That both incidents had happened because of a specific convergence of circumstances. Something was going on that was more than just psychosis or mental illness...

Mid-August 2004 – It had been an awakening experience, triggered by a dangerous combination of increasing yoga and mediation practice, combined with the use of mind-expanding drugs. Stand-out reasons for this included the blissful oneness I had experienced, the high level state of flow and intuition that had persisted for an extended time, the prostrations I had spontaneously performed, the strange language I had spoken, the snake's hissing voice I'd spoken in, the visions and intuitions I'd had, the energy that had snapped, crackled and popped up my spine, and the guidance that had led me through it all.

That experience, kick-started at Shambhala Music Festival, began on the Sunday morning. With a quarter tab of Acid. And a yoga class. I only made it halfway through the class – I remember going into Lion's Pose, a yoga posture I'd never done before. The class was outside, on the grass, close to the river that flowed through the Festival grounds. We were kneeling with our hands on our knees, and the teacher showed us how to exhale forcefully through an open mouth with the tongue sticking all the way out.

Ah Acid and Lion's Pose... in the middle of Lion's Gate, an astrological phenomenon I knew nothing of at the time...

I remember doing the pose at least twice... AHHHHHH! And then I was done with the yoga class; even though the yoga class wasn't done. I stood up, rolled up my mat, and smiled at the teacher who frowned at me, confused. I ignored her and walked off, feeling like I knew... I just knew. What did I know?

Everything.

Simply everything.

I had accessed Infinite Consciousness.

The second experience – mid-September 2004 – had been triggered by extreme internal resistance to my fiancé breaking up with me, backed by a childhood pattern of emotional suppression working in overdrive and causing extreme disassociation and then delusion. This had likely been exacerbated by my already weakened psyche from the first experience, which caused me to totally lose the plot.

Drug-induced awakening and severe emotional trauma.

As long as I steered clear of both of those potentially triggering things, I was confident that I wouldn't experience psychosis again, medications or no medications.

So I began, with the support of my friends and Mum, to wean myself off.

I also started working again – as head bartender for a swanky upmarket $1000-a-night hotel. It was jarring, working in an environment with drunken people, as my increased-sensitivity had left me with no tolerance for drunkenness anymore. Or maybe I was just triggered because carefree drunkenness was no longer an option for me.

Eight months after being committed to the psych ward, I saw the possibility of getting my life back. Not there yet... but it was glinting in the distance. If I could just keep moving. Which I was. Some sense of deep internal grit was driving me forward – that, and a strong sense of knowing.

I wasn't kidding when I said that the Universe had wrapped me in its sweet embrace and whispered all its secrets into my ear.

It had.

All of them.

I knew everything.

Everything.

Heaven is a Place on Earth

Laingholm, 2017

B ut knowing everything, then, was not enough. Because, similar to right now, contemplating the unfolding connection with my ex-lover/lover, I still don't know so, so much. My own unconscious attachments and fears block me from perceiving clearly.

That's the kicker – access to claircognizance, the gift of knowing, is blocked by one's own fear and attachments.

And anyway, knowing everything wasn't enough back then, either. Back in Whistler, in 2004.

It was not enough to keep me in the blissed-out state of awareness and flow that accompanied that first awakening / psychosis. It was not enough to stop the onslaught of intense emotion that accompanied the second psychosis. And it was not enough to allow me to hold on to the life I knew and loved.

And, when I came back to New Zealand, it was not enough to keep me from falling right back into unconsciousness again. An awakening can only be sustained when the foundational psychological clearing work has been done before. And I had done shit, really. Oh sure, a bunch of yoga and meditation. But not the sustained, daily, integrated, guided practice that's required to undo the conditioning of a lifetime, or more. Awakening or not, I was right back where I'd started, trapped deep within Maya, the illusions of my conditioned mind.

Sure, I had a reference point for what life could feel like – without drugs – when one was totally present, heart-centred and in flow. When one was awake. I'd had that glimmer in Hawaii in 2000, after the healing session that had initially triggered Kundalini, even though I didn't know it at the time.

But that wasn't where I was now. Instead, post second-psychosis, I was in a fear-based, shut down and contracted state of being. And the contrast between that, and being in total present, heart-centered, flow state was extreme.

It felt like the difference between heaven and hell. States that are, just as Jesus said (and Belinda Carlisle) – places here on Earth. They are states that live within us.

Formerly, when I lived in hell – for hell it was – I was blissfully unaware that I was experiencing hell. Although I always knew that the fact I enjoyed taking drugs so much pointed to some underlying issues that would one day have to be faced. Because when life feels amazing – heart-centred, connected and flowing – there's little desire or need to do drugs. They actually lower your state of vibration. Drug use – and addiction in particular – seems to be related directly to trauma. Heal the trauma, and the unconscious need driving the drug use will drop away (although there can still be mental habits or patterns which also need to be addressed).

That day of facing all my underlying issues came after the second psychosis. It came after I went back to New Zealand and ended up at my grandparents' house after my failed attempt to resurrect normal life in Auckland in November 2004.

It was like waking up and discovering that every unfelt emotion from the past 29 years, and every suppressed thought, had been dumped onto the floor of my living room. And the only way to find my way to the door – the door that led back into Heaven – was to sort through, feel and experience all the feelings and all the thoughts from my entire life and beyond.

The awakening that I'd experienced opened me into the Universe's loving embrace, to understanding and knowing everything there was to know... before ripping me back down into mental and emotional purgatory.

Which is exactly why there is a very specific process that yogis use to prepare the body – physically, emotionally, mentally and energetically – for the onslaught of Kundalini pulsing through the system.

Ah, yes – Kundalini. The divine feminine force of the Universe. She, who lies dormant, coiled at the base of the spine three and a half times around… until awoken. And then she begins to move. Ideally, if all the mental and emotional blockages (samskaras) have been cleared out of the systems, and the nadis (energy channels) are clear… Kundalini will shoot directly up the main channel – Sushumna – and exit out the crown chakra. Hello enlightenment.

That's not what happens for most people. And it's not what happened for me.

Instead, when the clearing and preparation work has not been done, and Kundalini awakens, anything that has not yet been dealt with is hunted down and thrust into one's conscious awareness for immediate attention. And life's circumstances will conspire to bring ALL of one's shadows, unconsciousness, fears and beliefs to the surface, one by one. Sometimes two by two, or three by three.

This has been my lived experience over the past 13 years.

And sometimes it feels like no sooner do I become aware of, and clear, a deep childhood trauma than something else pops up, clamouring for my attention.

* * *

And so here I am, in 2017, living in Laingholm, Auckland, and still excavating all kinds of wounds and traumas. Because Kundalini awoke within my system before I'd done the preparation work required to clear out the shit.

Last week, triggered by moving into yet another new home, the intense and unfelt emotion I'd experienced as a child around no longer having a home after my parents' divorce finally surfaced. And I finally felt all its multi-layered levels of pains. Feeling it meant tracking backwards and forwards though my life to see how unconscious desire and unfelt feelings had driven so many of my actions…

51

I made the unconscious, conscious. I felt the feelings. And I held myself through all of it. Now, those historical emotions had finally cleared.

Relief.

But not for long.

Because already, something else is going on.

I barely had time to sit in the sunshine and wallow in contentment before it was on to the next thing... dragged forward by the evolutionary pressure of Kundalini, seeking to clear out my system for total enlightenment. Or something like that.

Or maybe I'm just fucked up and will always have these crazy experiences of mood swings and intense feelings and total existential angst.

Nah... that ain't true.

At least, it doesn't feel true... because while the intensity of my emotional life has continued unabated since 2004, my ability to hold myself and contextualise what is occurring has increased by a multitude.

No longer do I drown in overwhelming emotion like I did that night in Auckland November 2004, hunched over and sobbing at the end of the bed.

Now, when I'm hunched over and sobbing at the end of the bed – like this afternoon – there is a steadiness that accompanies the anguish. I both witness myself and feel myself. I hold myself and sob myself. And once it's done, there's always a new insight and understanding accompanied by a sense of something clearing.

There, that's done!

Plus, perhaps most importantly, I have now cultivated a variety of friends I can reach out to who understand exactly what I am experiencing.

I reached out to one of these friends this afternoon.

"Having a hard time at the moment. Experiencing a total loss of confidence in everything right now. All constructs are melting away. What is real? How do I engage with anything?"

Her response could not have been more reassuring and supportive.

"I'm in an 'existential angst' period too. It feels like a ... loss of faith in everything."

Phew. I'm not alone. Thank God.

Because that is probably the hardest aspect of this path. Of any path.

Aloneness.

Being the only one.

Not having anybody to reach out to.

* * *

Queenstown, 2005

It was my girlfriends at the Lily Pad in Queenstown who gave me the foundation to get back on my feet and working again. While neither of them had ended up locked in a psych ward, they'd been through shit too, and we'd lived the same life in Whistler. They made me feel somewhat normal again.

Even as I realised that I was no longer normal.

That this awakening had forever changed me.

Even my perception had changed – there seemed to be a new way of "seeing" that had opened to me, and I didn't know what to do with it.

My boss at the fancy pants hotel in Queenstown would be detailing the issues with last night's bar closing... and I would drop into a no-thought space of listening where it felt like another dimension opened up within reality... and my vision changed... and all of a sudden everything was energy. It was a state where knowingness surged through my cells and I could feel the masks he wore and see the beliefs that drove him, and his actual words about the bar faded into the background as who he truly was pulsed forward energetically.

WTF?

I shut it down. Made sure I didn't listen in that way. See in that way. Because while this is a useful skill when leading retreats – seeing people's masks and beliefs is what that game's all about – it tripped me the hell out way back then in Queenstown 2005.

As did the drunk people, because I couldn't handle them any longer either.

53

I felt their angst, and their unsaid thoughts, and their hidden hearts, and it was all too much to handle.

So I quit the head bartending gig at the fancy pants hotel after a brief three-month stint. And landed a freelance writing gig within the week that gave me just enough money to pay the bills.

Way to call in what's needed.

* * *

But then, unwittingly, I called in a new boyfriend. Only a week after my ex-fiancé – we'd been talking regularly since I'd landed safely back in New Zealand – declared to me over the phone that he couldn't live without me. That he was going to move to New Zealand, marry me and have my babies.

It was what I wanted, right?

But I started crying as soon as I got off the phone. I cried all afternoon – it was Sunday and I wasn't working – and I cried all evening. The next morning, when I was still crying alone in the kitchen of the Lily Pad (the other girls were at work), I called a girlfriend and she immediately came up to the house.

"But I thought that's what you wanted?" She asked, bewildered at my ocean of tears.

"So did I!" I sobbed. Yet even though it was what my mind wanted – even what my heart wanted – my body knew the truth. I couldn't take back the man who had abandoned me at my weakest. Who had rejected and left me after that first awakening and psychosis. I felt betrayed and I couldn't trust him again. He couldn't hold me, and I needed to be held, in both my shadow and my light.

The tears were the realisation of that truth. Until that moment – when he'd declared he was coming – our growing re-connection had all been a convenient fantasy lived out on the phone. He gave me enough love and support to keep me going, without me having to face the reality of being in an actual relationship with him.

I called him back. Said I couldn't do it. He hung up on me. And we didn't speak for at least four years. That was when he went and found my girlfriend and they started going out – my vision realised. Did I cause it? Or did I intuit it?

Meanwhile, without a man in my life, I was unconsciously shit scared. Yep, totally driven by fear – there's another example. Something I didn't come to realise until many years later. But I did notice that there was barely a week in between saying no to my ex-fiancé and yes to an old friend.

He was in London. We started texting. And talking. Three months later he came back to New Zealand. We moved in together. We got engaged.

I felt safe.

But it was never real.

It was all about safety, all about not being alone, all about someone I trusted taking care of me. Being with someone who could hold me. It was probably no coincidence that he was physically the most imposing and impressive Adonis-like man I'd ever been with.

See, despite everything that had happened – all the visions and insights and understandings and knowings that had surged through my system – I was still acting from deeply buried unconscious shit. And every time I acted from fear, I caused suffering in my life and in the lives of my lovers.

After that important year with my girlfriends at the Lily pad, I rented a house with this man, and we even got married, in 2006.

We threw an engagement party – a superhero engagement party – and dressed up as Mr. and Mrs. Incredible. It seemed the perfect costume for his physique and my yoga-obsession. And then we pulled out a marriage celebrant halfway through the party and got married on the spot.

The next morning, – the morning after our wedding night – he awoke to see me sleeping on the floor, because he'd gotten wasted, passed out and fire-trucked the bed. Or pisscapaded as the Canadians say. So he got up and put on a suit and started drinking for breakfast.

He knew.

I didn't love him.

I was using him.

I was unconsciously using him for safety, because he had a big heart, and because I could trust him, and because he truly cared.

I denied it, and I tried, with everything I had to love him back, but it was never going to roll. No matter how much I WANTED it to…

Fifteen months later, in 2007, I moved out of our bedroom and into the spare room, where I slept for a month. Accommodation in Queenstown is notoriously hard to find, and I was loath to leave our home – which I loved. Another relationship, another home, another breakup.

Then a fellow Toastmaster asked me out on a date. (Yes, I was going to Toastmasters, brushing up on my public speaking skills.)

But I couldn't go on a date while I was still sharing a house with my ex.

So I found a room in a house in record time, and on my birthday, helped by Ange, my Lily Pad girlfriend, I moved everything I owned to the new house. We celebrated with champagne in the hot tub, toasting to my big date, organised for the next night.

This was it. I was still writing – freelancing enough to get by – and I'd started teaching yoga at the local gym, and then a friend's studio. Three years out from the Lion's Gate Hospital's Acute Psych Ward and I was beginning to feel mostly normal again.

Maybe I'd finally made it.

I mean, I didn't cry as often, except on my yoga mat. I was doing work I loved – teaching yoga and writing. I'd even met a Swami who had confirmed – finally! – in person, what I'd only ever suspected. That my experience wasn't just psychosis and that I'd had an awakening. Swami Shantimurti had given me some practices to do, daily. That gave me the hope and validation I'd desperately been seeking. I'd also started a blog called *Be Conscious Now* and was attracting a growing audience, talking about my experiences of Kundalini Awakening and psychosis.

I had a foundation to build on, an understanding of the experience I'd been through and practices to help support my healing.

This was it.

I was on my way.

The only way was up.

The next night, August 4th 2007, I went on that date, with the man from my Toastmaster's Club. And so began the most debilitating, confusing and abusive relationship I had ever encountered.

Hello Rebel Heart Warrior

Laingholm, 2017

This morning, I was driving the Auckland motorway, to drop my son at the airport, so he could go see his Dad for the school holidays. And finally, breakthrough!

Yes, breakthrough.

Thank fucking God.

Because sitting in the shit, mired in fear, sobbing my heart out, unsure of what's going on, unsure of what to do... sucks arse. Big time. Especially when there's this voice inside your head saying:

"Look at you, 13 years of hard work and processing and healing and releasing and you're STILL in this place. Maybe it's all a load of bollocks. Maybe you're all a load of bullocks. Maybe you don't know anything at all and you're just very fucked up. How the fuck can you lead retreats, teach yoga, post on social media. Who the fuck do you think you are?"

That voice might be faint, barely audible, even with the super-sonic hearing I seem to be left with post-2004, but it's still there, reaching out to me and threatening to drag me down at any moment.

And there's nobody to save me from that damn voice. Nobody but me.

Because that's the thing about this awakening journey I've been on, hard out, since 2004. There hasn't been any ONE person to guide my way, day in and day out, year in and year out. No consistent teacher, no guru, no one who's been there, done that, and can provide context for each pile of shit I find myself in. When someone did show up – like

Swami Shantimurti – I never ended up working with them consistently over a period of time.

Instead, it's been me, every step of the way, staying anchored to the witness through my dedication to yoga, and practicing relentless self-care no matter what. I'm the one who has pulled myself up by the bootstraps, refusing to believe the doctors waving their prescriptions and diagnoses (but smart enough to keep my mouth shut and do exactly what they said until I got my sorry arse out of their care and back to NZ).

I was able to do this because of that knowing I spoke about – a deep inner sense of truth that has been with me since that first awakening / psychosis. And I've been able to do it because of this particular voice inside me. A voice which I first identified when I was in the psych ward, the second time around – the time they committed me to incarceration until I was proven sane.

Let me tell you about that 'voice'.

Whistler 2004

An acquaintance from Whistler – she worked at a hair salon a close friend also worked at – happened to drop in and see me. At the psych ward. In Vancouver. The ONLY person who dropped in and saw me other than my soon-to-be-ex-fiancé (that I remember). Not only did she come and see me, but she brought me a journal.

"I know you love to write and I thought this might help your recovery."

Angel.

Right there.

And there have been plenty of angels who have dropped in and cared for me and guided me in the last 13 years.

Fuck, I'm tearing up now, sitting at the wooden dining room table here in Laingholm, just remembering this angel. I don't even remember her name. Yet her small act – HUGE act – of kindness may have been the thing that saved my arse. Because that night I wrote my three pages of Morning Pages, a practice I'd been doing for years (at all times of the

60

day) since reading *The Artist's Way* by Julia Cameron. I wrote those three pages and at the very end I wrote:

"The sun will again shine on my life so THERE."

Defiant. Determined. Resolute.

Despite being locked in a psych ward and apparently mentally ill.

Laingholm, 2017

I feel that energy inside me again, now. That was the breakthrough that happened today after dropping my son at the airport. I was still mired in fear, locked into conditioned mind, feeling like shit. While driving into Auckland to show my campervan to a potential buyer, I was stopped at the traffic lights and my eye caught a sign on a truck.

"Witness."

It was a brand, or something. But witness – yeah, of course. Witness.

Just that one word was enough to shift my state of awareness from being mired in the shit to watching the shit.

I need to watch my thoughts – because I am not my thoughts. That's another thing I've known deeply since going crazy, because when I was going crazy, I wasn't. That is, the part of me that was true was watching the part of me that was thinking all kinds of crazy things. I was witnessing my mind. And if I'm witnessing my mind, then who the hell am I?

Which is why it's a misnomer to say: "She lost her mind."

Bullshit.

We don't lose our minds, ever.

Our minds take over the show and we lose our centre. Something the yogis call the Atman – that which we really are.

So there I was, this morning, driving along the motorway, feeling like shit, and there it is emblazoned on a truck beside me.

"Witness."

Okay, message received.

So I begin to witness more deeply what's going through my mind. And as I do, I recall what happened yesterday morning. I'm on the phone to that ex-lover/lover of mine who's all of 12,000 miles away. I'm meant to be prepping to teach yoga but I'm in the emotional quagmire and have decided it's more productive to get him to take me through a process so I can get through the shit and pop back up again into awesomeness.

Only it's not working. I can feel some part of me resisting him, resisting the process. I don't want to do this. It's too painful, too fucked up, too hard.

"Witness."

That's resistance. That's a part of me blocking myself from getting back into awesomeness. What part of me would block that?

Threads begin to weave together.

That resistance. Blocking me. And how damn ineffectual this state of being has made me over the past week. All the shit that's been going down in the world out there – police violence, a mass shooting, politicians being fuckwits in the wake of environmental devastation. And me, too fucked up to BE anything that might shine a big enough light to counter some of that darkness.

"Witness."

I'm driving, and so I start to witness. And as I start to witness again, I see it. Fuck, I feel it.

I'm fucking afraid. So fucking afraid right now. So, I name it. This is one of the most powerful actions you can ever take – naming what is. And especially naming Fear. Fear is only powerful in two circumstances.

1. When we feel it and are afraid to face into it.
2. When we don't know we're feeling it and delude ourselves into running from it.

It was the second circumstance that sent me spiralling into that debilitating, confusing and abusive relationship I'll tell you all about soon. That's unconscious fear. It's impossible to do anything about because you don't even know it's happening. Until you get really good at noticing the signs of unconscious fear, in the same way that we automatically recognise the signs of a strong wind. Suffering comes from unconscious fears just like trees bending and breaking are the result of strong wind.

62

And this morning on the motorway, witnessing that fear – that was the beginning of my breakthrough – witnessing myself in action. I saw that I was afraid. And I named that fear.

Okay, great, this is where I am. A-fucking-fraid.

Now, what am I afraid of? Because my life is pretty damn good. No one is shooting me, or bombing me, or hating on me. There is money flowing in from work I love, I live in a house I love with people I love and my family and friends are awesome.

And, even though my emotional life is intense, I'm not afraid of that. I've built up a huge amount of resilience and I can handle whatever emotional and mental turmoil is thrown at me – doubly so because I am using my skill at navigating this territory to work with other people, so saving them from suffering. Woo hoo! Less suffering in the world – that's gotta be a good thing.

Given all that, why am I so afraid right now?

Ah... sneaky... I see you! Self-sabotage. That's the layer at work right now. That's the aspect of Self that has grabbed the mic and been running the show for the past few days. The Saboteur feeds on fear, runs on fear, and operates from fear.

All the thoughts that have been spinning through my mind...

"I don't know what's real anymore. I don't know how to engage with life. I don't know who I am. I can't handle how violent and messed up other people are. I don't want to play this game anymore. I'm too far out from other people's experience for anybody to understand me."

These thoughts have all been couched in pseudo-spiritual terms. As if the reason I'm stuck is BECAUSE of the path of awakening. Awakening is the reason I'm all fucked up. And so, if I can't trust that, what the fuck do I do? How do I live this particular wild life of mine?

What a brilliant way to self-sabotage! See how damn wily the mind is? And I was believing it. I'd gotten totally sucked into the mind. I'd stopped witnessing, and started believing the bullshit.

Phew.

Big breath in.

Okay.

If this is true – that I'm afraid and sabotaging – then what?

I'll tell you what... I experienced a total 180-degree energy shift where all of a sudden I wasn't in the shit anymore. Nor was I afraid. And I certainly wasn't sobbing my heart out and unsure of what to do.

That shift got me right back in touch with my inner Rebel – if that's what you want to call that voice in my journal in September 2004. Because that was HER:

'And the sun will again shine in my life so THERE.'

Mania Stinks

Laingholm, 2017

I feel her energy, burning in my veins, that Rebel of mine.

Once, in Glenorchy earlier this year, I felt her so damn strong that she became totally personified. As if she was separate from me. As if she was some angel guide sent here to keep me on track. Early twenties, African-American, sassy as all hell, a couple of children already, an ex-slave even. And feisty, so damn feisty.

Medical intuitive and author Caroline Myss would call her an archetype. New Agers would call her a guide. It doesn't really matter what you call that energy – it's all just a construct, like everything else in this created world of ours.

We're making it all up.

And what we're all making up seems pretty hellish right now.

Because it doesn't have to be this way at all. We could be living in a completely different world – a world of peace, and love, and creativity and FUN.

This I know for sure.

And that's the certainty that I lost in the last few days. I got sucked down into my own darkness, my own private hell, by the aspect of Self that Caroline Myss dubs the Saboteur. That damn sneaky mind of mine.

But I'm back.

The energy switch between fear-based living and knowingness is so extreme – it's from one pole to the other. And yeah, when it's unstable, without context, and totally ungrounded, it could start to look a whole lot like the collection of symptoms known as bipolar disorder disorder.

After all, bipolar disorder disorder is characterised by swings from depressive to manic states of being.

I've been manic.

And I've been in kick-arse awesomeness and knowingness.

And they are two very different states of being.

They even SMELL different. Yep, mania has this certain essence about it – it stinks a certain kind of way. Mania is what happened to me during that second psychotic episode. Not the first – that was the awakening – But the second one that happened after my shit-scared fiancé dumped me. Can't blame him – who wants a crazy wife?

But mania never happened to me again. Not even when I went off my meds, slowly and under supervision, at the Lily Pad in Queentown, early 2005. But I did come face to face with mania again, in 2012.

Wellington, 2012

I was newly separated from that debilitating relationship you will hear all about, and now had a young child, just turned one year old. We were living with three flatmates on Happy Valley Road. A flatmate moved out, and an older woman moved in. About four weeks after she moved in, she shared some of her history, mostly because a documentary had just been made about her and was coming out soon. She'd spent most of her twenties – and then some – in psych wards getting all kinds of nasty and totally ineffective treatments, like shock therapy. And yes, she'd been diagnosed with bipolar disorder disorder.

We weren't fazed – I'd had my diagnosis. Another flatmate had ended up in a psych ward with psychosis after a Vipassana Retreat (ten days of silent meditation). Mental illness was the new black as far as we were concerned. Everybody has it; it's all in how you dress it up.

And then our new flatmate had a manic episode.

I came home after picking my son up from his dad's and there was a gathering in the lounge. Ruth (not her real name) was wandering around doing her thing while a support worker and friend kept one eye on her and explained the situation to all of us. Apparently, Ruth was in mania and needed to go into respite care – it was all being organised.

I was fascinated.

So this is what mania looked like from the outside?

It was eerily familiar – because I could literally smell it! I recognised an essence, and that smell.

At one point, I disappeared into my room to get something. Ruth followed me and stood inside the door staring at me.

"This is for YOU," she said. And then she was gone. This was for me? What? So I could better understand mania? So I could see that it had a certain kind of energy signature? How could it be for me?

Now, reflecting on that, I do wonder at the connections, at the unfoldings, at the synchronicities. It's almost as if Ruth knew I was called to write this book, and knew that her role was to show me what mania looked and smelled like…

But that's crazy talk right? How could that be so?

From what I observed though, living with Ruth for those few weeks, her experience made complete sense to me, within the context I'd constructed post-psychosis. My theory was that mania was a result of the sense of self or awareness fleeing from strong emotion in the body. And that in time, if that emotion isn't felt and released, manic episodes continue to happen because there is a 'path' worn into the nervous system and brain. That makes it more and more likely that this defense mechanism will be the automatic response to strong emotion.

Ruth was in her mid-60s and had a lifetime of patterning. And, a documentary about the shittiness of her experience was about to be released to the public, bringing up all kinds of horrible feelings and memories.

No wonder she went manic again. I saw her. I got her. Hell, I smelled her!

Thirteen years after my experiences and I'd never had another whiff of mania.

Until this June 2017, in Glenorchy.

When Relationship Becomes the Yoga

June 2017, Glenorchy

I was living with Tussock, my son's honorary grandfather. And I was fresh from breaking up with my lover from 18,000 kms away. One night and one day... I got a whiff of mania again.

But it never developed beyond more than a whiff, because of the two things that have defined my life over the last thirteen years of recovery.

Relationship and yoga.

In some ways, they are one and the same thing. Ask a freshly certified 200 hour teacher 'what yoga is' and likely they'll trot out the standard that 'yoga means union'. That's the intellectual understanding of yoga they've been taught. Give them time, and enough practice, and that understanding will deepen and become experiential. A knowingness of the truth of that definition will then permeate one's cells... and it becomes everything.

Everything.

Here I am, right? In here. And there the world is, right? OUT there. What lies between? Between the world and I?

Relationship.

What is relationship?

Perception.

I see the world, and believe it is as I see it.

Until I can begin to see myself clearly and realise that the world is as I am. It is as I see it through my filters and beliefs and ideas.

So too with the men in my life – for while all relationships in my life have proved fertile ground for growth over the years – it's been the romantic relationships that have sucked up most of my energy and attention, and delivered the most growth.

I adore men. I adore sex. I adore who I am in relationship to a man – I adore being the Lover, the Companion, and the Sidekick.

Yet, I have struggled – massively – to enter into and maintain loving, real relationships. And, I've even managed to spend three and a half years in a toxic relationship.

Yet, what is relationship but union? What is union but relationship? One flows into the other, becomes the other. When I practice yoga postures, it is not the shape I make with my body that is important, but the relationship that I'm having with the shape I'm making with my body. Until that relationship dissolves into nothingness and I become one with my body – no mind at all.

It is the same in relationship with the Other.

When we first come together with someone – fall in love perhaps – the energy that flows between Us and Them is defined by everything that is happening in our psyche and their psyche. It is defined by our beliefs about love, relationships and the world. By the ideas we hold in our heads. By the thoughts that we think when we see them, talk to them, listen to them, and be with them. And of course, by the feelings that we feel.

All of this – beliefs, ideas, thoughts and feelings – it all flows back and forth between us and creates The Relationship.

Of course, we're mostly unconscious of this flow. Until it begins to impede upon the relationship. Until it causes friction, or conflict, or a withdrawal of energy because we don't like what we're feeling anymore.

These are the Shadows. The parts of us we haven't owned yet, don't love, don't like, and pretend don't exist. Our weaknesses, our neediness, our failings, our triggers, our traumas and our ego defences.

It was my Shadows that psychosis dumped on my metaphorical living room floor in the guise of boxes and boxes of unfelt experiences I'd been stuffing into the psychological basement for years. And so, after that experience, after the Awakening, it was Relationship that I used to begin to see, heal, release and love my Shadows.

Which is why the toxic relationship, which began on August 4th, 2007 and lasted until December 31, 2010, was such a powerful vehicle of growth for me. And it's why am I so grateful to the man who walked that journey with me. Because in his reality and in his story, I was the toxic one.

We functioned as dark mirrors for each other – revealing each other's unconsciousness, fears and shadows in all their awful glory.

Thanks to my growing dedication to yoga, which became a daily practice when I started teaching in 2006, I was able to use this relationship to become a better version of myself – but so very often, a toxic relationship can suck the life out of us.

This use of relationship as a vehicle for awakening is Yoga, as self-realisation, in every way. Specifically, it's Tantra Yoga. We're learning how to welcome every aspect of ourselves, to sit with it all, to love it all, to be with it all. We're healing all of this – all of this stuff that is not who we are.

And that's the process of awakening.

Because while you could say that I'd had an awakening experience in August 2004, it was only a few fleeting moments of a random collection of energetic phenomena and a taster of pure bliss and oneness. It was not abiding, nor did it positively impact my psyche in any way, other than a brief but powerful experience of the Witness and of knowing.

That awakening didn't lead to enlightenment. It was just the first step onto the path. Or maybe the second, or third.

* * *

Many people who experience Kundalini Awakenings have no idea that it is just the beginning of the process – that now the real work starts. Now the HARD work starts. That now you MUST do the practice and turn inward, investigating every thought, every action, and every behaviour so you can understand where it's coming from. That's the relentless self-observation. That's the Yoga.

I discovered, in my practice and in my Yoga, that nothing was more powerful, in helping me make my unconscious conscious, than relationship.

And on my journey of relationship, I discovered that nothing was more powerful in helping me love more fully and more clearly than Yoga.

Yoga, intertwined with relationship, became the perfect crucible for waking up and for working with Kundalini. It couldn't be any other way. One feeds into the other.

Which is why this story – of Kundalini Awakening – is about both yoga and relationship. They are one and the same thing.

So, let me tell you a story. It's a story that will bring you up to speed on my long and varied romantic history. Some of this I've already touched on, but this will give you the full meal deal.

* * *

Once upon a time there lived a young woman who felt unseen and unloved. Possibly she was only imagining this, and she was both seen and loved, just not in the way she knew was possible.

Most nights this teenaged girl, after writing faithfully in her diary, would turn off the light, close her eyes, and disappear into a world of her own making.

This world was almost identical to the world she lived in now – she walked to school, she caught the bus into town with her girlfriends, she hung out at the beach – but in this world, invariably, she always had an encounter with a handsome young man.

They would meet – he would approach her – they would begin to talk, possibly they kissed, and sometimes events progressed all the way to passionate lovemaking. But not often. It was the meeting that she laboured over, that she wove elaborate stories around. This, and the imaginary conversations that she and these mysterious young men had as they saw her, appreciated her, and then fell in love with her.

Like the Hollywood stories she'd soaked up, and the fairy tales she had read by the thousands, the young woman assumed that these stories all ended happily ever after. It was simply the meeting that was important. Beyond that, everything else was always taken care of.

When she was 18 years old, in her last year of high school, this young woman fell in love, real world love, for the first time. Out with friends one night, cruising in the back seat of a car, she spied a young man on the side of the street and something in her woke up, opened up, sat up, and... that was that.

It turned out that this young man was the cousin of the car's driver, so they swung back around and stopped to chat. She got his number – or he got hers – a phone call was made and the next night he showed up at her house to hang out. And the night after that, the night after that, the night after that, and... six consecutive nights later they were going out.

She had met her man.

They were in love.

The fantasy had come true.

Unfortunately, what the fantasies and the Hollywood stories and all the fairy tales had failed to provide were instructions for navigating the territory of relationship. She was clueless. He was clueless. And all the love in the world couldn't keep them together.

They broke apart one year and two months later. She had headed to the Big Smoke for the summer, excited for adventure after a conscientious and hard-working year at University. The plan was to have some fun, sow some wild oats, and then return to settle back into her loving and committed relationship. If she was honest – and she wasn't then – she wanted to experience different kinds of sex. She just knew that the kind of sex they were having wasn't all there was... and she wanted to see what other men were like.

She didn't notice or hear her boyfriend's anxious response to this plan. She was too oblivious, too cut off from her own emotional landscape, and his. Too hell-bent on living life her way.

So, she went, unaware that she was breaking his heart, expecting to saunter back into his life three months later and pick up where they'd left off, with plenty of letters and long-distance phone-calls in between.

They did write. And they did call. Until he called and told her he'd met someone else.

"But I haven't slept with her – we've just been hanging out."

"I don't give a fuck if you've fucked!" she screamed down the phone at him. "It's your heart that matters!"

But she'd broken that heart already and he'd talked himself out of their relationship, citing her desire to travel and roam the world wild and free sans-children, and his conflicting desire to get married and have children.

"Married! Children! We're only 19 and 21!"

It was too late. He was gone. And she was bereft. But she didn't know it. As she had always done, and would continue to do for another decade or so, she stuffed the emotions into the dark depths of her unconscious and rationalised that she didn't care and it was better this way anyway.

A month later, due to fly back to her hometown for her second year of Uni, she spontaneously decided to move permanently to the Big Smoke.

"Intuition and guidance!" she proclaimed, unaware it was actually avoidance and denial. Going home would have meant coming face-to-face with her ex-boyfriend and his new girlfriend, soon to be wife and future mother of his children. Staying in the Big Smoke would feed the fantasy that she didn't care because she was having the time of her life, adventuring around the world.

And so began a 15 year period of almost constant back-to-back, long-term, monogamous relationships. She loved men. Men loved her. And she had this deep conviction that the love she had once fantasised about as a teenage girl was somewhere out there waiting for her. And the sex. If only she could find it... find HIM!

Boyfriend #2 began as a close friend, progressed into a friend with benefits because the sex was fun and adventurous. After much cajoling from him – and unconscious rationalising from her – he become her boyfriend. She followed him to London, to France and finally to Whistler. But with such a shaky foundation it was no surprise, even to her, when everything imploded in the dark silence of non-communication.

Mercifully, she managed a solo break here for two years. She lived it up in Whistler, dallying with this man and that as she pleased but reserving her heart for no one.

Until she met Boyfriend #3, and through a haze of Black Russians and lines of blow fell madly in love, as if she was 19 years old again. He loved her too – adored her, madly. And they managed to hold it together for nearly three years in a web of co-dependence by unconsciously tiptoeing around each other's insecurities. Her sexuality threatened him and so she kept suppressed it to keep him happy. But there was only so long she could endure this suffocation, and when she finally exploded out and began to live from freedom again, it was over within 12 hours. He got triggered, which was not in her fantasy script so she didn't know how to handle his anger. Feeling like the only way to be with him was to cage herself, but no longer willing to trade love for freedom, she bolted.

Straight into the arms of Boyfriend #4 who had been circling in wait, knowing that Boyfriend #3 wasn't going to last.

'You're too good for him."

At last! A man who adored her. And even better, wanted her to be free. So free, in fact, that he was happy to invite other people into their bedroom. She could be her wild sexual self and still be loved! And their sex life was powerful, deep, raw, a creative connection she'd been searching for since she'd left Boyfriend #1 at 19. She'd finally found the man who could meet her sexually.

This time, it was her insecurities that got massively triggered. Her inability to speak her truth that shut her down. Her intuition said that if she did speak up, if she did stand in her power... he would be gone.

So she choose, again, to cage herself, again, and became a shadow of her former Self – an insecure, weak, and needy shadow. Boyfriend #4 baulked, promptly fell out of love, and dumped her.

This time she paid the ultimate price for decades of denial and avoidance, and splitting herself into mind over heart. You already know what happens next.

Yep.

Psychosis.

Twice.

For the first time since she had fled home at 19 due to the heartache of Boyfriend #1, at 29 she returned home to New Zealand – to her mother's house. She was broken hearted, broken minded, and, facing the complete shattering of her life, she sought comfort wherever she could find it.

Alcohol and substances were off-limits due to the fragility of her mind, so she found this comfort in the texts of an old high-school friend who materialised at exactly the right time. He was living overseas now, and in the dying throes of his own relationship. She supported him and consoled him. He made her laugh, he lightened her darkness.

Within a matter of months, he'd returned home and become Boyfriend #5. Yet again, the foundations were weak. He was afraid that she didn't really love him. She knew she loved him deeply, but suspected she wasn't IN love with him. She felt safe with him – cared for, loved. But she made him feel inadequate. She was an intellectual, concerned with the nature of reality. He was a tradesman who delighted in adrenaline sports and motorcycles. They had different interests and saw the world in different ways. And she squirmed when they had sex – that deep energetic connection she'd had with boyfriend #4 was missing and after experiencing those heights and depth of connection, a purely physical connection seemed pointless.

It couldn't last, even as they tried with everything they had to hold it together because they were old friends with a long history. Within 18 months, they too had parted.

Just in time for Boyfriend #6 to waltz on in and ask her out on a date. A date! She went. They laughed and talked and flirted. You might remember how that went! He charmed and seduced and shone bright. She went home with him that night and moved in two weeks later. All the while knowing that this wasn't a smart move. All the while feeling ashamed at her weakness with men. All the while sensing that she needed to stop and look at her patterns to better understand what was going on with her and love and men.

The wheels fell off fast. Oh, the love was there – deep, passionate, soul-expanding love. But so too was manipulation, verbal abuse and emotional abuse. Yes, she found herself knee-deep in a swamp she'd never experienced before – the dark, dank, sucky-ness of an abusive relationship.

And she was stuck in deep. Not only did she allow him to persuade her to quit her teaching yoga – her soul's calling! Now she was broke, relying on him for money while he bad-mouthed her friends. Ashamed of the tight timeframe between Boyfriend #5 and #6, she isolated herself.

She tried to leave, and he sweet-talked her back. The love was mind-blowing. And the sex was effortless and connected, an energetic dance between two souls that knew each other. The abuse was devastating. He wanted to head to the Big Smoke so they could seek their fame and fortune, and so she agreed. She ignored the fact that she seemed to be the one that did everything – searching all over town for an apartment they could afford while he disappeared off into the backwoods with his family.

Holed up in a one-bedroom apartment, riding the waves of good times and abusive times, the young woman despaired. How had she ended up here? She had great self-esteem! She loved herself!

Torn between his love and his abuse, she flipped a coin. Stay or go? Stay or go? Every time, it flipped up STAY. And she knew why. She couldn't fail at another long-term relationship. She was now in her early thirties and this was her sixth long-term relationship – the fourth, back-to-back, within ten years.

The common denominator in all those relationships? Her.

And so one evening, after he'd fallen asleep drunk and stoned, yet again, she fled to the bathroom to sob. Curled up on the cold lino floor, she made a vow to herself.

She would never fail another relationship. She would stay in this one until she figured out what she was doing wrong. She would find her way into the kind of relationship that she knew was possible – the kind that Hollywood wrote about, that fairy tales celebrated and that she had once fantasied about as a teenage girl.

She would go the distance and find her happily ever after, so she could one day sit on the porch with her man and watch the world go by, content in the knowing that she was loved and that she loved.

Somehow, no matter what, she would find a way.

* * *

Relationship is the Path

I t was nine years ago that I made that vow and it took another two and a half years for the relationship with Boyfriend #6 – Mr. Toastmasters – to successfully conclude.

I say successfully, because by the time I chose a different experience, I was well along the path to becoming more conscious in relationship. I had learned how to love unconditionally – although it was still a work in practice. I was beginning to step into my power in relationship – learning how to tell the truth about what I was experiencing rather than editing it for fear of losing the relationship. With practice, I was getting faster and faster at catching myself when I slipped into unconsciousness and 'forgot' to speak truth.

That combination of factors meant that when relationship #6 ended, it ended from a place of power, truth and love. On my side anyway.

Because when I stood in truth and love, the only direction to take was away from the relationship. Under the blazing light of truth and love, the relationship evaporated.

Not because I had failed, as I had in every other relationship. Failed to communicate properly, failed to listen properly, failed to love unconditionally, failed to be truthful, failed to stand in my power... but because I had succeeded.

Coming out of this relationship, I took a vow to stay single for at least six months, so I could get clear in my own power. No more running from one relationship and falling into the next.

Six months to the day, the exact day, I was asked out on a date and my next relationship began. Only this time it was different. I didn't merge completely with the man, nor lose my centre in my deep desire for oneness. I paid attention to those moments when I strayed from truth and brought myself back as fast as possible. I noticed when I loved conditionally – wanting him to be other than he was, holding back, getting sulky. And instead of this turning into another failed long-term relationship, the truth of our connection was revealed in less than six months. We parted ways as friends, knowing that we weren't for each other.

I felt proud of myself because I could sense that I was progressing. That something had shifted in me.

The next relationship lasted only three months and contained even deeper truth and love. I noticed that my intense desire to be with someone meant I jumped into relating with people who weren't fully aligned with me. That there was attraction on one or two levels: sexual and intellectual, or sexual and heart, but never all three – sexual, heart and intellectual.

I realised that more discernment at the start would save heartache along the way. And I also recognised that every relationship I experienced was revealing more of my shadows and leading to greater freedom and insight within my psyche. I was waking up and becoming more conscious, relationship by relationship.

This time, I was single for over a year. The growth I felt myself experiencing meant that there were less and less men that I related to, and I began to ponder whether my level of consciousness meant I would ever meet a man who could match me. There's that subtle ego-trip again – the Saboteur.

One early morning walk in 2013, across the Glenorchy Golf Course, feeling into this, I realised that my own freedom, or liberation, was more important that being in a relationship. If it was a choice between romantic love and self-realisation, how could I choose anything other than self-realisation?

So I let go of my desire for a relationship…

…and promptly met my next boyfriend, discovering that I wasn't nearly as conscious or awake as I'd thought. I still had plenty of fears, insecurities, projections and shadows swirling inside me, the difference now was that my ability to witness myself in action meant that these fears, insecurities, projections and shadows became more quickly apparent.

It also meant I became more awake to the dynamics within relationship – to the subtle ebbs and flows of the unconsciousness of my partner. And I began to realise that it was impossible for me to be with someone if I couldn't share what I could see and feel. Yet in this relationship, this man wasn't ready to hear those insights.

We parted.

And that was the last short-term relationship I had until I met Mr. Europe three years later. Certainly, I experienced plenty of crushes along the way, which led to the cultivation of excellent friendships with many of these men. But I never again felt the need to enter into a short-term relationship with a man in order to live out the dynamics that revealed my shadows.

Actually, Mr. Europe had entered my life a number of years before, still married at the time. We were both writers for *Elephant Journal* and I'd interviewed him for my website, *The Yoga Lunchbox*. After his marriage ended, we became friends via Skype. He was there, listening, through many of my dalliances with men, and my experiments with using relationship as a way to wake up. I was there, listening, as he ventured back into dating and relationship after eight years of marriage.

Finally, we conjured up a reason to be in the same physical location – I invited him to lead a retreat in New Zealand. We co-facilitated that retreat and our connection was obvious, although we were both unsure about what form the connection would take. I desperately wanted Mr. Europe to fit in with my idea of romantic relationship, while he was unsure if he could commit to one woman.

So we didn't know, but I was hoping. We did know we had something worth exploring, and we believed we had the tools and awareness to do the exploring by embodying unconditional love and truth at all times. We thought we could apply the right tools and strategies to the challenges that arose, because we both knew our relating would call forth all of our Shadows.

That began a year of the most intense growth I've experienced. There was no longer anywhere to hide, at all. Mr. Europe triggered all of my relationship issues. He called forth my shadows on a consistent basis, allowing for ongoing integration and greater wholeness. The relationship itself became the cauldron for making the unconscious, conscious – it became the fire in which all that was false burned away leaving nothing but the truth that is the hallmark of waking up.

It seemed I could have both – romantic love and Self-Realisation. I didn't have to trade one for the other. And in fact, one *was* the other – there was no separation. Relationship became the way to enter self-realisation just as self-realisation was the way to enter relationship.

I thought I'd finally made it. I thought I'd finally met the man I could walk this world with... but of course; I couldn't see what I couldn't see. There was plenty of unconscious shit going on with Mr. Europe and I, right from the start, and I was mostly blind to it. Although some red flags did pop up along the way.

It really felt though, like I might have finally found the Holy Grail. Because of all the things we can attain in our modern life, a loving, intimate relationship is the Holy Grail. To love and be loved, see and be seen, hear and be heard, know and be known, understand and be understood. We want to be accepted and acknowledged for who we are, as we are, in all moments.

This is our deepest desire, although we don't always know it.

Stepping into this kind of relating can hurt like hell. Opening fully to love another without conditions means that whatever is in the heart – old wounds, ego defences and trigger points – will be felt. It cannot be avoided. Yet in the feeling of those triggers – as I was to learn – we find liberation and ever deeper intimacy and love.

Which is why, when Mr. Europe chose to spend the night with another woman, it triggered the end of our romantic relationship in that moment – but it didn't trigger the end of our relationship. It broke my heart, and it opened my heart even more.

He and I continued to relate to each other with love and truth, even though we were no longer romantically together.

The shape of our relating may have morphed and changed, but the underlying love and truth that made up the fabric of our relating was still intact.

At least it was, until I broke his heart again. But that is still to come…

Yes, I know – none of this really explains how relationship and yoga saved me from mania.

But it's coming... I promise.

The Root of Mania

Glenorchy, 2017

That stench of mania wafted through my life again in mid-June 2017, a few weeks after Mr. Europe had chosen to spend the night with another woman. He'd been unaware and unconscious of the heartache this would cause me, and that – true to my word – it meant that I would choose to end our romantic relating.

We kept talking, often, as we navigated the shifting form of our relating.

But it was painful. It was really fucking painful.

The night he told me, the morning after he left her apartment, I got fucking angry. And I hung up the phone. It was morning for him in Europe, evening for me in New Zealand. But before he rang, before we spoke, I already knew. I'd known all day, in my body. I could feel it. My body has this way of feeling the future. Or feeling what's happening, 18,000kms away. There is a nervous system response and emotional response even though the events haven't occurred yet, or haven't been revealed to me. So I was ready for the call.

The moment I hung up I stared at the phone and then dialled right back. I determined in that moment that I wasn't going to run from this pain. Instead, I decided to step into the fire and feel it as deeply as I could, as fast as I could, and burn through it at light speed.

That's how I've done everything since we've been together. Since we *were* together. Three days shy of a year, plus four years of long-distance friendship before that.

He answered straight away and I laid it out, "I'm going to need to fully feel and express everything that comes through me right now, and

I want you to hold space for me. Don't take anything personally, don't defend, don't explain, just let me do what I need to do."

And he agreed. Because this is what we did for each other in that year of romantic relationship – we held space while we each worked through our triggers and our trauma and our issues. It's what we both do in our professional lives as well and we're fucking good at it, separate and apart. It's one reason our connection is so mind-blowing – we got each other on the deepest possible level, and we were always there for each other, loving each other the best we can.

So he listened as I sat on the edge of the bath, wrapped in a blanket to stay warm because the heat of the wood-burning fire in the lounge didn't reach the bathroom. He listened as I got angry and screamed and yelled and said some unkind things. And then, after I'd crawled into bed when the chill of the bathroom became too much (and because all I wanted to do was curl up into a scrunched-up kitten-sized ball and make myself invisible) he listened to me sob for what felt like hours.

That was the first phone call after it happened. For the next few days – week maybe – we spoke every day, sometimes twice a day. That's what we'd done for the last year too.

We'd had to – because of that 18,300km that separated us. We needed to speak that often to build and maintain intimacy. And to make sense of our worlds, to hold each other as we'd grown and changed and evolved.

And, right from the beginning, Mr. Europe had been honest with me about how he felt. Or didn't feel. From the first time I came to see him in Europe, in August 2016, he'd been telling me that he wasn't sure if we wanted to be with me. That he felt like something was missing, that he might want to be free to be with other women.

Be with other women? That was fucking hard to swallow.

We were sitting on a blanket, under a tree, soaking up the August sun outside the cabin in the woods that he'd rented for my visit. As soon as he'd finished telling me, his phone rang. His wife... Ex-wife.

I left him there, on the blanket, and wandered up the banks of the hill opposite to find another tree to sit on. Leaning back on my haunches, feeling my ankles opening and hips opening, I observed my internal reactions.

I mean, there I was, 18,300km away from home. I'd ponied up a bunch of money, left my son behind, and flown two days around the world just to spend two weeks with Mr. Europe in order to see what we had and if it was worth pursuing. And on Day #3, or something like that, he drops this bomb.

"I don't know what I want... I don't know if I can commit to just one woman..."

I squatted under that tree, and breathed, and contemplated. What response was truth? What was unconditional love? Could I hold him in his truth without betraying mine?

My heels dropped deeper into the squat the longer I sat there, as his conversation with his wife/ex-wife went on.

It seemed there was nothing else to do but accept him and the situation as it was. Right now, he was only with me. And he didn't know, for sure, what he wanted.

And that gave me hope.

I walked back down the hill and surrendered to this not knowing, and I continued to make shit happen so we could come together. Because I'm good at that – making shit happen. Like retreats that brought us together in Bali, Mexico and New Zealand, and another trip to Europe, with my son this time.

18,300 kms?

Phesh, I wasn't going to let that stand in our way!

And so I didn't, and our relationship rolled along. Except for the fact that Mr. Europe still didn't know if he wanted to actually BE with me, that he still felt like he might want to be with other women, or even have more children. And I just kept holding space for that, until he knew.

He never did know.

Instead, one week after saying goodbye to me in Auckland after another five week New Zealand visit, he went out and spent the night with another woman.

And then I knew.

I was done – with our romantic relationship anyway.

At first, after he spent the night with another woman, and I said I was done, romantically, he tried to pull the enlightenment card on me.

Said that I was loving conditionally – on the condition he wasn't with anyone else.

Said that I was loving from a place of fear and attachment – fear of him being with someone else, attachment to the idea of being together only with each other.

Said that I was less awake.

I'd been walking around the Glenorchy Lagoon when that conversation took place. Slow, measured steps along boardwalks over wetlands and streams, my gaze taking in the muted greys and browns of the winter landscape, blood running cold as I listened to him tell me I was less enlightened than him because I wasn't okay with him sleeping with other women.

Hearing that bullshit was fucking hard – I felt unseen, unheard, misunderstood and bullied. These were things I'd never felt in our relationship before. The very bedrock of our relating was built on seeing, hearing and understanding each other's realities deeply.

And all of a sudden, it felt like we'd hurtled back into some old paradigm style of relating where he was trying to convince me of his way and his perspective as if there is only one reality.

I got angry then. I needed to get angry – to assert a boundary. I'd stomped and kicked my way along the walk, deliberately keeping myself firmly in my body to give myself the courage to speak truth in this moment. I wasn't going to be railroaded again by a man attempting to get me to behave the way he wanted me to behave. In my world, there was nothing un-evolved about the choice I was making to contain sexual energy in a particular way. It fucking pissed me off that he was co-opting enlightenment to try and coerce me into his way of thinking and seeing and believing.

Fuck that shit.

I'd been here before, in a relationship with a man I'd loved deeply, who had also wanted to be with other women.

At the time, I thought I wanted that too. I thought I was totally into multiple partners. And I tried my hardest to force myself into being that woman, the one who was sexually open. Who was polyamorous.

And I couldn't do it. The lack of congruency between what I was feeling and what I was attempting to do was a major contributing factor to my psychosis, which came at the tail end of that relationship. Then, I was so absorbed in my internal experience I'd barely been aware of the landscape around me – the mountains that rule over Whistler.

Now, here in Glenorchy, in June 2017, I was intimately aware of their presence and power. The Glenorchy mountains lined the West, presiding over the township and lake like a Council of Elders. I looked to those mountains for support and grounding as I navigated the end of my relationship with Mr. Europe.

A year had passed since Mr. Europe first shared in August 2016 that he might want to be in an open relationship. I'd been feeling into my desire to be in a contained relationship and I wanted to be sure of where that desire was coming from. I wanted to know that I could trust my own knowing, that I could stand in my truth and say, THIS, for me.

I'd done the work. And by the time Mr. Europe spent the night with another woman, I knew for sure. I want Sacred Monogamy, and only Sacred Monogamy.

This is my expression of life.

This is who I am. Or at least, who I am choosing to show up and be, in this infinite wonder of life.

But despite that rift – the way it ended and our differing views and desires on relationship – Mr. Europe and I continued to speak almost daily. And through that, my heartache and grief and disappointment over his inability to fulfill a particular role for me – that of romantic partner and future builder – eased and left in its wake a profound gratitude for the love and connection we'd shared.

At that time, in June 2017, no one knew me as deeply as he did, nor understood the self-realisation work that I was doing so profoundly. Mr. Europe too has had a Kundalini Awakening. He too has experienced depression, anxiety, bliss and everything in between. He too has taught yoga, and understands the path of Self-Realisation.

And so it was Mr. Europe I turned to that June when mania knocked on my front door for the first time since 2004.

It was a Monday, and for almost 36 hours I'd been experiencing a whiff of mania – a subtle stench wafting up from my unconscious.

At least, that's how my perceptual reality might be described in the Western medical model – mania. There were also huge amounts of creative, positive, excited energy flowing through my system. But those weren't what concerned me – I'm used to having this level of joy pulsing through my veins. It was my lack of groundedness and centredness that freaked me out.

And what freaked me out the most was that it felt like my centre of awareness was constantly being yanked out of my body. As if I were being pulled away from myself by something 'out there'.

This feeling was new. Different. And it was strong - real, real strong. Was I being pulled out of my body by some unseen force? Or was I trying to flee my body because of some deep emotion ready to surface?

Yoga practice helped, when I snatched a moment at 6pm to sit and do it. But it was short-lived. As soon as I got up and about again, doing the bedtime routine with my son then cleaning the kitchen, the sensation of being pulled out – way, way out – of my body returned.

Part of me was fascinated by the subtle sensations. I felt myself tracking them, even as thoughts raced through my mind.

'I'm sure this hasn't happened to me since I got back from Canada. Is this an opportunity to observe the beginnings of mania and understand exactly what's happening on an energetic, subtle and psychic level?'

That curiosity was accompanied by fear – I didn't want to lose my ground and float away into the ether. And I sure as hell didn't want to go into psychosis again.

And so when I got on the phone to Mr. Europe after my son was in bed, I laid out in brief what I was experiencing and ended with a plaintive; "Help!"

Mr. Europe was brisk and got down to business straight away, honing in on my breath and some of the visualisation work I've done in recent days.

"Cut that shit out, for now."

I heard him. Meditation can exacerbate Kundalini, and it can also exacerbate mania. Kundalini and mania might be two very different states of being, but sometimes they can both be fuelled by the same thing.

Talking to Mr. Europe was incredibly helpful. Just feeling the centring and grounding in his energy helped me to find the same in mine. Call it mirror neurons if you like, call it clairsentience. But I was able to bring my energetic state of being into vibration with him. I could FEEL his centre, feel HIS ground, and by centering my awareness on his centre and ground, it triggered a sense of my centre and ground.

And so, after that conversation, I slept well that night – despite the slight mania – although it took me about forty minutes to get to sleep. And the next morning I walked, outside, in the rain, before having a cooked breakfast.

All of these things – a friend I can rely on, healthy sleeping patterns, walking in nature, eating well – are crucial to my well-being. They're non-negotiable. It's just how I live my life, no matter what. I've reached the point where I'm highly attuned to my energetic state of being so at the slightest shift – like that subtle edge of mania I could perceive – I'm able to recalibrate as needed.

I don't think about any of this. It's automatic. It springs from a deep knowing of what it is I need to thrive, and a deep caring for myself – I value giving myself what I need to thrive.

It's possible that if I hadn't slept well, if I hadn't eaten, if I hadn't gone outside into the elements and walked for an hour or so... the mania might have grabbed a stronger hold on me.

But it didn't. Those actions helped to keep my awareness firmly IN my body.

The strong state of Witness that I'd built up over the past 13 years also meant that when I felt mania tugging at my consciousness I was able to witness it, name it, and respond to it instantly with self-care behaviours designed to ground me. I wasn't caught 'unaware'; I wasn't unconscious of what was happening to me and within me. I recognized it, instantly, and I responded, appropriately.

But none of that was what shifted the mania completely.

And without shifting it completely, it would have continued to ebb and flow within my consciousness.

I was determined to get to the root of what was CAUSING the mania to flare up, because I had a theory that if I could release the root, it would stop it coming back, completely.

That's the context I'd wrapped around my experience of mania since 2004, and now I had an opportunity to test out my theory on a real, live subject.

Me.

I'm a One Man Woman

T hat theory needs some background though, before I can flesh it out for you. So let's go back to Vancouver in September 2004 – the Acute Psych Ward in Lion's Gate Hospital.

There I am, in a single bed beside the doorway leading into the corridor of the Ward. There are three other beds in that room with me. I feel her now – that woman, me, waking up for the second time in a psych ward. Only this time, she's not waking up from a bad acid trip, with her fiancé sitting anxiously beside her. She's waking up alone and remembering that he's left her, that there were no drugs to blame, and that she's all alone.

I can feel myself, then. That moment of coming-to and everything flooding back into my mind and into my heart. Into consciousness. I was emotionally distraught, but trapped; because there was no way I could allow myself to be vulnerable in front of strangers. This was one of my deepest unconscious fears – I was scared to be vulnerable. And so I was caught between my need to feel and my fear of feeling.

So I couldn't cry. I couldn't allow all the emotion in my heart to be felt, to move, as I desperately needed it to.

And this time, because I couldn't blame the drugs – the only drug I'd ingested in the previous four weeks was the medication I'd been given the first time around. That terrified me – if I could 'lose my mind' and it wasn't because of the acid, or the mushrooms, or the weed... What was it from? What had triggered it this time?

Emotional upheaval. Being dumped by my fiancé. Life.

Just. Fucking. Life.

And if life could trigger psychosis in me so easily, did that mean there was something seriously wrong with me?

Was I mentally ill? Was I bipolar disorder? Was I fucked up? Maybe there had been no awakening after all.

Terr-i-fy-ing.

* * *

Then, that woman I was… in the psych ward that second time… was also so unaware and unconscious of what was going on in her emotional landscape. Only her behaviours and the train wreck she'd made of her life had the ability to reveal the truth.

Now, I'm highly attuned and aware of every tiny internal shift – thanks to relentless self-observation, born of a desire to wake up, fuelled by a fear of going crazy again.

Because I never did go crazy again. Not once in the last 13 years. Those were the only two times that I experienced psychosis. Although… they weren't the last times that I experienced trance states similar to the trance states I entered into during the awakening experiences.

In the past two years in particular, I've learned how to journey deeper and deeper into trance states in a way that allows me to access and process the deeper, darker corners of my psyche, and also to access the collective unconscious.

I've found myself in eerily similar situations to my psychosis, only completely anchored, centred and sane. And, if someone was there with me, I would be able to give a blow-by-blow description of what I'm experiencing internally, like a scientist observing a science experiment.

Case in point. I'm in Auckland, in Newmarket. I'm driving out of a car park to head back to Laingholm to pick up my son from school. It's an everyday, mundane activity. Only I'm hit with a strong wave of Kundalini energy, and then suddenly I'm channelling a masculine energy through the right side of my body. It's a strong wave – my right lip curls up, my face changes shape and I feel malevolence echo through my body.

I know this energy. It's been coming through me since Mr. Toastmasters and I lived in a damp, one bedroom flat in Newtown. It's an energy I used to see move through him as well. Is it him? An entity? A physical representation of an emotion?

I don't know. This is a tricky landscape to navigate and there's no one guiding my way. And, until now, I've been hesitant to reveal too much of what I experience because people might think I'm crazy. Or bipolar disorder. Or schizophrenic. Or experiencing a multiple personality disorder.

I'm none of that. And I know it. These experiences come through me – they are not WHO I am. And as long as I stay anchored and connected to that which I truly am, I'm okay.

By the time I hit Motorway 16 going west, the malevolent masculine energy had faded. I note as many details as I can about the experience, collecting data, looking to learn what I can so I could better understand the experience. Field notes – science.

Because that is what I am – a scientist – and my internal landscape – my body, mind, emotions and energy – is my laboratory. Of course, it's impossible to be objective. Yet science is now proving that subjectivity is all we really have, and that the mere act of observing something changes the thing being observed. Objectivity does not exist. Instead, I prefer to examine my experience through the lens of potentialities.

So that strange energy I experienced that day – potentially it is an entity that I first witnessed in somebody else, and that entity can now enter my energy field. Potentially it isn't an entity, but the energy of that person. Potentially it is the physical manifestation of a particular kind of emotional energy. Potentially it's some kind of energetic hallucination and I'm just making shit up. All potentialities are possible and I attach to none of them… although I have preferences for one or two.

And that may be the distinction between a crazy person, and a person who experiences life in a multi-dimensional manner beyond the norm.

Crazy means believing your own shit and becoming attached to something being true. Navigating the multi-dimensional nature of life with maturity means being willing to examine everything and attaching to nothing.

I experience life in a different way from most people. This does not make me mentally ill. This makes me super fucking sensitive. Gifted. Talented. A seer. A medicine woman. Clairsentient. Clairvoyant. And possibly clairaudient. I'm definitely claircognizant – bring on all the Clairs!

* * *

It's frightening at times though – both the multitude of energies and realities I experience, and the way that I cycle through intense emotions as I process the past of my experience, the now of my experience and sometimes even the future of my experience.

Yet I've also become fucking amazing at it. I am a highly skilled emotional processor, and this skill is what makes me an amazing retreat leader. I'm able to feel what's happening in other people's psyches and to guide them with a light touch to process their own experiences.

At the time of writing, I was still having moments of doubt. Big moments of doubt. Moments where I'll have been feeling like absolute shit for days – mired in deep fear, unable to access the root of the distress – and I'll start to wonder, "Maybe there is something wrong with me. Maybe I do have a medical condition. Maybe I am bipolar disorder! FUCK!"

But then, something will break open – I'll get to the root of the fear, I'll be able to fully feel it and release the insight that deep fears always contain, and I'll break through and up into the light again. More whole, more integrated, and more wise.

Phew! Made it!

After a while, thanks to my relentless self-observation, I began to pay close attention to those doubt-fuelled fears: "Maybe there is something wrong with me. Maybe I do have a medical condition. Maybe I am bipolar disorder!" And I noticed, by paying close attention, that those thoughts invariably preceded a big breakthrough by about 24 hours.

Now, when those thoughts float through my mind, instead of believing the thoughts or even wondering if they might be true, I feel excited, because I know I've almost made it through this particular emotional process. I'm just 24 hours out from a big breakthrough. Stay the course, almost home again.

Now that's progress.

* * *

Back to Glenorchy, in June 2017, when I almost experienced mania for the first time in thirteen years.

After the phone call with Mr. Europe, where I shared the reality of the mania I was experiencing, and after journaling about the subtle sense of mania I was experiencing, something shifted internally.

That's not unexpected. Being witnessed and naming shit is a big part of the healing process. Healing isn't a complicated business – it begins by simply acknowledging and naming what's happening. For me, that often means journaling it out. Or writing an article, or a Facebook post. Witness the hundreds of articles I wrote between 2008 and 2016 as I navigated waking up via my website *The Yoga Lunchbox*.

But, even then, the work was far from complete. There's more to healing than acknowledging and naming what one is feeling or experiencing. And that Monday in June, in Glenorchy, was a big workday, which meant I didn't have time to go into the next stage of healing required. Instead I had to attend to multiple phone calls as I organised retreats, immersions, a trip to Auckland to check out a school for my son, booked flights, handled emails, edited a client's book, and wrote my own. By 3pm I was exhausted and wrung out in a way I hadn't been for months, because I was internally pushing away the healing that was ready to happen, while pouring all my energy into my business.

And then it was time to pick up my son from school and be fully present for him. As I pulled on my boots, jacket, scarves and gloves to brave the two-block walk to Glenorchy School, I felt distraught. I didn't have enough in me to parent properly – I'd spent everything I had on work and now I desperately needed to do my practice and lie on my bed and stare at the winter sun dancing on the wall.

My needs had to come second though. My breath crystallised in the air in front of me as I plodded down the road. It felt like I was crashing. Was I crashing? Was this what happens after mania?

On the way back, Sam in tow, I was honest with him about my capability to play that afternoon, even as I made an effort to simply be present with him. And somehow, we made it through the afternoon. He constructed a sporting arena built with cardboard and held together with the help of a despairingly messy glue gun before dinner; afterwards we played a game of chess.

Tussock, whose house we were living in, adores Samuel – has ever since Sam was a baby, back when Tussock used to board with my Mum. Sharing a house with Tussock was a godsend for me because we shared the cooking, housework and Tussock had things I would have been unlkely to own, like glue guns.

One of the things they loved to do together is read – in the six months we were there over the winter of 2017, Tussock read Samuel the entire Harry Potter series. I was in on it at the start, and loved reading the stories out loud to Sam, but somehow it became the thing they did together and in the end, I left them to it.

That difficult day, after dinner, Tussock and Sam dove into Harry, and so I grabbed the opportunity to dive into practice. Finally.

I rolled out the prayer rug I was favouring over my yoga mat in the small space at the end of our beds, lit the candle on my altar, and sat down with a blanket draped over my knees and one around my shoulders.

It was Day 481, Take #2 of my 1000-Day Practice. During practice, as always, I examined my body, mind and emotional self to see what was going on, post-mania release. Where was I? Who was I? What was happening inside?

Breathe, move, breathe, chant, breathe, and meditate. Breathe…

The mania was gone, completely. A relief. Instead, there was sense of heaviness and a slight depression. I'm used to working with depression now, and have become lightning-fast at getting to the root issue of my body's depression response. See, in my experience, depression occurs like some kind of drag or resistance. It means that there's some emotion beginning to surface that I don't want to feel, or some aspect of my life that I don't want to look at.

Depression is a symptom of that desire to avoid. It's not the thing itself, simply the symptom.

Sitting in meditation that June evening, I used my breath to hone my awareness ever deeper into myself. What's giving rise to the depression? That was my question.

Emotion. There it was.

Grief.

Sadness.

Okay, what's the emotion related to?

A thought exploded up from the depths: 'I don't want to do this all alone. I don't want to face this all alone.'

Okay, great – now I was getting somewhere. That thought pointed to the resistance I was experiencing.

See, I was alone in that moment. Yes, I had support in my life – witness the sound of Tussock reading to Sam in the lounge right now. Witness the deep emotional support Mr. Europe was offering; witness my extensive network of friends and my close-knit family. But I didn't have a partner standing beside me, sharing this life and facing into this with me. Not when Mr. Europe and I had just broken up, two weeks ago.

A thought arose.

'I want a loving partner to go through life with.'

It was authentic desire, welling up inside me as I sat on my prayer rug listening to the hum of the heater and Tussock's lilting southerner accent through the walls.

'I want a loving partner to go through life with.'

I allowed myself to fully feel that – yep – emotion.

But my alarm for meditation started going off and it was only ten minutes before Samuel's bedtime and I needed to step back into the role of Mother.

Emotional processing had to wait, so I hit pause internally. Progress had been made. The rest could wait.

And it did – until Mr. Europe and I spoke later that evening.

In the conversations that he and I had during our year together – on the nature of relationship, on enlightenment and waking up, on what we want to experience in life – Mr. Europe constantly questioned my desire to be with a man and create a future with that man.

"Attachment," he'd say. Fear-based. Old paradigm. Conditional. Love means being free, completely, to explore whatever comes along.

That conversation has been a defining thread in my life – witness my first long-term relationship where I felt it was perfectly reasonable to go off and sow my wild oats before coming back into committed love. Witness my relationship with my fiancé, where his insistence on sharing our bedroom with other people felt like it aligned with my deepest truth. Even though it didn't, at all.

And then, while being with Mr. Europe for that year, with him unsure if he wanted to be in a monogamous relationship, I'd had an opportunity to fully examine all my ideas and beliefs around relationship.

Was I coming from attachment? From fear? From deep unconscious social conditioning?

I questioned it all. I felt into it. I ran scenarios in my head. I explored the idea of being free to be with other men.

In short, I did the work.

That June evening, post slight-mania, feeling into the strong emotion deep within, accompanied by this thought: "I want a loving partner to face into life with," I felt like I'd tapped into an authentic desire that I always knew was there, but could never quite feel.

Now, I could feel it. I could own it. I just knew – this mattered to me and it was okay to claim this.

Finally!

After all these years of exploring myself and men and relationship and desire, and being with men who want to be with other women...

Finally!

I know what I want and it's okay to want what I want.

It's okay to want what I want.

It felt big. It felt powerful. It felt real. Like claiming something that I've been afraid to claim.

I'm eager to share this insight with Mr. Europe, to proclaim to him that what I desire is O-fucking-K. So after I put Sam in bed, I take my phone into the bathroom where I can talk in private and, lying on my rug for warmth, I lay it all out for Mr. Europe. I'm in tears as I do so – deep tears, open tears, vulnerable tears.

I'm telling Mr. Europe, this is the truth of my life.

I want a man to walk beside me in this life.

And as I'm telling Mr. Europe, I'm realising that this is what I could never own when I was with my fiancé. This is what I could never tell him. Because I was afraid that if I did tell him, it would be the end of our relationship.

Fear. Right there. Afraid of speaking my truth.

My fiancé was clear, when we got together, that the terms included threesomes, or partner swapping, or swinging, or something. And I agreed, whole-heartedly, mistakenly thinking that this was what I wanted too.

As our relationship progressed, and I realised with horror that including other people wasn't what I wanted, I felt trapped. I couldn't back out, because I believed I would lose this man I adored. But I couldn't bring myself to bring other people into our bedroom, although we tried, twice.

Flashbacks: to a night when we brought a couple home. She, a slight blonde with an air of fragility and vulnerability. He… I don't remember him much, just the lavish way he leaned over and moved one of my limbs so he could have a better view while his wife and I made out on the bed.

It was enough. I leapt up. Grabbed my clothes.

"I can't do this."

I scuttled down the stairs of the open lofted bedroom and huddled at the bottom feeling dejected and miserable because yet again I'd failed to please my fiancé. He'd come down and tried to convince me to come back up. Memories flood my system of that moment – me, wordless, shaking my head. His disgust as he went back up the stairs to let the couple know we were out. The way he ignored me when he came back down.

I tried… and failed, multiple times.

That conflict between who I was, and who I thought I needed to be to keep my man happy... that conflict put enormous pressure on my psyche and was a major contributing factor to my psychosis.

So on that cold winter's night in Glenorchy, after Mr. Europe and I had broken up because he chose to be with another woman, there I am, experiencing a do-over. That is, a moment in time that mirrors an earlier experience in my life, only this time I'm not wordlessly shaking and huddled at the bottom of the stairs. This time I'm able to stand in my power and, with love, state my truth.

I'm a one-man woman.

Mr. Europe hears what I'm saying, and he understands, even though it may not be what he wants to experience. He gets me, and holds me in my emotional space, tears and all. We may have broken up, but fuck do we love each other through this time in our relating.

I'm wobbly when I crawl into bed that cold June evening. There's still more emotion percolating under the surface of my awareness and I can feel my reluctance to move toward it. This surprises me – in the last year in particular, I've eagerly turned toward any hint of buried emotion, knowing that it always leads to release, healing and insight.

Not this time. I note the internal reluctance. Do I really have to go there?

I turn over in my narrow single bed, my queen feather duvet doubled up on top of me, weighing me down and creating a cocoon that insulates me from the -5 degree Celsius nights that are all too common in Glenorchy.

Fuck. I have to do it, I can't not cry when there's emotion there. And so the tears begin to fall, silently. My son is asleep an arm's length away from me on a single trundle bed. And through the wall, Tussock is also sleeping. Silent crying is one of my skills however, and my shoulders heave and shudder as the emotion comes through.

It's still uncomfortable. It's still odd. Why am I crying? What does this emotion relate to?

In the oceans of tears I've cried in the last 13 years, there have been lakes and lakes worth of unknown tears for unknown reasons. And possibly lakes worth of tears that are not even mine – at times I've felt like I was crying out the pain of the world.

Tonight though, it's personal, I can feel that much. It's mine.

Snot runs down my face and I'm loath to wipe it on the sheets, which aren't due for changing yet. Washing linen is time consuming when almost everything has to be dried on the small drying rack over the fire.

Tissues. I had a packet the other day. They were in the lounge, and I cleaned up and brought them back into the bedroom...

I scoot a hand out from under the duvet and land directly on the tissues in the corner by the wall. Prayers are uttered for divine flow. The universe has my back.

After blowing my nose, I find myself huddled in a ball on my right side, and deep shudders wracking my whole body, as if I'm trying to make myself invisible.

A thought cracks through from my unconscious.

"I don't belong here."

This is the process. Feel the emotion, release the thought or the insight, and so understand the psyche.

"I don't belong here."

That thought time-travels me back, hurtling through years and then a decade and I suddenly know where I am and what's happening.

"I don't belong here."

I'm back in the psych ward.

These are the tears I couldn't shed when I landed in the psych ward, the second time around.

"I don't belong here."

I surrender deeper, and deeper, and deeper, allowing myself to sob it out and blow it out for at least twenty minutes before the wave finally subsides.

Connection made. The truth I could never speak to my fiancé, the emotion I could never feel in the psych ward. All coming on the edge of a wave of slight mania. Mania that is now gone, completely.

The mania came because I was resisting feeling emotion – a small part of my psyche wanted to flee from the emotional reality inside of me. That's what I experienced mania as – a flight from emotional reality into the safety of disassociation.

My awareness of that process, combined with my ability to catch the state of being I was experiencing, meant that I was able to coax my Self back into my body and into the emotion that was ready to surface. And once I did that, I was able to go into the tears and feel what I could never feel then.

My theory held up – at least in this very small case study. I was able to apply my hypothesis that mania is an expert defense mechanism against deep, painful emotion, and so can be disarmed by staying in the witness and feeling the emotion.

This is healing, on a deep level.

This is how I have recovered from two episodes of psychosis and a diagnosis of bipolar disorder.

This is how I have lived my life since 2004.

Honing my awareness, bringing my unconsciousness into consciousness, feeling whatever needs to be felt, holding myself with love through the entire process.

I have never worked with a psychologist, or a psychiatrist, although I did see a counsellor for a couple of sessions. But as a result of the work I have done, I understand the vagaries of the psyche intimately. And more than intellectual understanding, I can FEEL the workings of the psyche, intimately. Not just mine, but other peoples' too. It's a learned skill that has served me well as a yoga teacher and retreat leader.

Or perhaps it's a born gift and talent that I've always had, and which set me on this path in the first place.

Because can you imagine being a 4-year-old little girl, or a 7-year-old-little girl, and being able to feel the truth of people's psyches? A truth that was, in most if not all cases, very different from the words that were coming out of their mouths?

Can you feel how disorienting and confusing that must have been?

Possibly, that is why I completely shut down my emotional reality as a child, never to feel anything until I was in my mid-20s and using mind-expanding drugs.

It was those drugs that began to explode cracks in the armoury of defences I had built up since childhood – defences designed to stop me from feeling anything, because I felt and intuited too much and I couldn't cope with it all.

If relationship and yoga practice have been key elements in my recovery from psychosis, so too have drugs.

Only that's not quite true.

It's not the drugs themselves, but the context within which they are used, and the relationship one has with them.

We're going to need to talk about drugs.

But not just yet. First, lets talk about context. Because context is crucial when it comes to drugs too.

I Am Not My Mind

Yes, context.

That's what I want to talk about now.

Context and relationship.

Because it's context and relationship that create reality, and give us power.

It was context and relationship that made all the difference in my experience of psychosis and my recovery from it.

Right from the beginning, I knew that what had happened to me was not random, nor was it just "mental illness". I knew it wasn't an imbalance in my brain chemistry, nor was it genetic patterning. All of those apparent causes placed my experience outside of my control, as if it was just something that happened TO me... and there was nothing I could do about it.

Well fuck that. It's my psyche, my experience, my life... there's got to be something I can do about it.

And there was – I created a context that allowed me to constructively work with my experience in a healing manner.

I knew that if I could track back from the moments of psychosis and discover what had led to those thoughts of craziness, that I could then heal the trauma at its source. I knew that all I had to do to heal was understand the WHY. Why did I have crazy thoughts? What was the cause? Because every effect has a cause.

And that includes apparent biological effects. My brain on depression, or on mania, might be biochemically different to your brain in 'normalcy', but my sense was that to put the biochemical differences at the root of the experience was backward. They weren't the cause – they were the effect.

I knew that relentless observation – yoga – while holding myself in unconditional love – the witness, also yoga – would allow me to do this work of understanding how my mind worked and why it went into psychosis. And that was how I chose to relate to my experience. That was how I chose to use my experience – as fodder for waking up, or self-realisation.

So... context. Create your context. Own your experience. Facilitate healing.

Here's what I knew way back then in October 2004, when I arrived back in New Zealand to begin the healing process:

I knew that two separate yet intertwined things had happened to me.

I'd had an awakening – huge amounts of energy pulsing through my systems that had blown open the doors of perception and given me access to all kinds of information. It felt like I'd been given a key to infinite wisdom and knowledge and it was all flowing through my system. Every song, every book, every movie, every TV show, every religion, everything humanity had ever constructed or created. Known. Accessible. Available.

And I'd witnessed the strong defence patterns of my ego attempting to control and manipulate reality in a way that was inconsistent with the external data, because it was attempting to keep me safe. Because it had identified feeling strong emotion – such as grief – as 'not safe'. This was the psychosis.

Awakening.

Psychosis.

Intertwined.

Yet not the same.

This gave me a twin focus for my experience.

I could continue to walk the path of awakening while exploring and understanding Kundalini from the inside out.

And I could examine and explore the workings of the psyche and trauma from the inside out. Be a scientist in the laboratory of my mind and body. Which is all yoga really is.

Turns out that these apparent twin focuses on the process of Kundalini and the process of psyche and trauma were one and the same thing.

Navigating my own healing path of recovery through the landscape of psychosis and a classification of bipolar disorder also meant that I was adamant about the following:

Don't buy into the Western Medical Model of context.

Don't believe anything my mind says without thoroughly examining where that thought comes from – what gives rise to it.

Don't identify with my mind.

Don't identify with my thoughts.

Don't identify with material reality.

Don't get sucked into creating and bolstering any kind of ego identity.

Here's what I made sure to do:

Practice yoga every day.

Eat good, nourishing, grounded food.

Spend time walking in nature daily, if possible.

Spend time bathing and soaking in water often, if possible.

Cultivate authentic and deep connections with people who understand awakening.

Make self-care a priority.

Prioritise making time and space for being with oneself.

Keep all commitments to a minimum so as to have space to be with volatile emotional states as necessary.

Prioritise being well.

Prioritise recovery.

Prioritise mental health.

Witness myself in action, and inquire into all thoughts and feelings when necessary.

Pay close attention to external circumstances and what they might reveal about my unconscious self.

Use all relationships as a mirror to see my unconscious and shadow self.

That last DO was my saving grace during the toxic relationship I entered into three years after psychosis, with Mr. Toastmasters. It's how I was able to live through what turned out to be the most confusing and abusive relationship I ever experienced, and come out the other side healthier than when I went in.

I kept asking myself, when Mr. Toastmasters appeared to do and say things that were all fucked up. "How am I fucked up in this moment? What is my side of this dynamic? What am I bringing to this?" And then, when I could see an aspect of my unconscious, of shadow, or fucked-up-ness... that's what I turned towards to heal next.

Over, and over and over again. Because I know Mr. Toastmasters found that relationship just as toxic and just as confusing as I did. Hell, he had a much clearer view of my fucked-up-ness than I did.

Because we're all fucked up. We all carry wounds, and shadows, and fears, and unconsciousness. It's what we do with our fucked-up-ness that is important.

Which is why my relationship with Mr. Europe was so extraordinary and so powerful. Our context, right from the beginning, was waking up. That was our focus – using our relating to see ourselves more clearly and wake up. Using the tools of truth and love to do so.

And that was why we were able to successfully navigate him choosing to be with another woman and me ending the romantic relating, yet still stay connected to each other. We never projected onto each other. We never blamed each other. We just saw the other as they were in all their fucked-up-ness... and held them in truth and love.

I knew Mr. Europe had unconscious weaknesses with women. I knew, because in some small way, I used those weaknesses as a way to get close to him. I could feel his neediness, and I responded to it. So, damn straight I was afraid that other women would be able to do the same thing. I knew what he was like.

And in the same way, Mr. Europe could feel how my unconscious fears were making me cling to him. He could feel my neediness too.

Because despite our high levels of awareness and our desire to use the relationship to wake up, we still managed to be co-dependent.

When Mr. Europe chose to be with another woman, it was exactly what I needed to finally get clear and stand in my power about who I was and what I wanted. It was exactly what I needed to finally trigger and feel into the deep pain and grief from waking up in the psych ward the second time, emotionally bereft after my fiancé had broken up with me. Because I didn't get sucked into any drama about what was happening with Mr. Europe and I — no blame and shame and pain — I was able to simply work on what came up for ME because of what was happening between us.

I worked on my shit, while he held me in it.

And Mr. Europe worked on his shit, while I held him in it.

We came back together in July 2017, in Mexico, to lead retreat together. We had two days together beforehand — the first time we'd seen each other since he'd been with someone else. We had those two days, and then we were leading a weeklong retreat for 14 people, with six days of wind-down afterward.

Challenging right? Yes, but totally possible. I knew exactly the context I wanted to create to make this retreat work. In the first two days, I wanted to clear out any residual anger and resentment that I might be holding that would prevent me from being fully present with Mr. Europe as a facilitator on the retreat. Those two days were all about me doing the personal work necessary to create the best retreat experience for the 14 people that signed up. During retreat, it was all about them. And after retreat, it was about Mr. Europe and I firmly establishing a foundation for our future relating as friends. Because I loved this man deeply and I knew that the connection we had was powerful.

We might want different things in life, but we were still going to be in each other's lives, even if only as colleagues and co-workers.

So began the most intense two-week healing period of my life.

And the most active Kundalini phase since 2004.

No surprise that these things would be so tightly woven together — Kundalini and healing. It's what the entire journey has been about, ever since Kundalini first moved in me. And that's why I've had no choice since except to face into the reality of my existence on all levels - mental, emotional, physical and energetic.

111

Nothing can be avoided.

Nothing can be suppressed.

Nothing can be hidden away.

The very purpose of Kundalini is to bring everything into the light where it can dissolve – all of our fears, all of our insecurities, all of our beliefs, all of our patterning, all of our identities, all of the roles we play, all of who we think we are. Until nothing is left but...

But what?

What is left when all of that is gone?

Who are we underneath it all? Underneath our fears and the ego defences they give rise to? Underneath our insecurities and the masks we wear to cover them up? Underneath our beliefs and the world we build upon them? Underneath our patterning and our identities and our roles?

What lies beneath?

There is only one thing.

And it is the same thing in everyone.

It is consciousness.

Pure awareness.

The, "I AM."

It is that part of me that watched herself in the Pemberton Medical Clinic and knew that something was wrong, yet was unable to do anything about it.

That is the only thing that is real – consciousness – because it is the only thing that is unchanging.

And when I am deep in the shit, mired in fear, sobbing my heart out, unsure of what's going on; unsure of what to do... it's all because I've lost touch with that part of me. With the real. With consciousness.

This is the journey.

From mind.

Into consciousness.

From hell – because make no mistake, a life lived from the mind, in the mind, by the mind IS hell – into Heaven.

This is the context within which I saw my awakening and my psychosis. It showed me heaven and it showed me hell. I knew myself as mind, and I knew myself as consciousness.

I wasn't crazy.

I was experiencing crazy thoughts.

Consciousness can never be crazy.

And I AM consciousness.

Except when I forget, and start to believe the thoughts that my mind creates.

But even then, I AM.

I've just forgotten.

And during those two weeks in Mexico, Mr. Europe and I did healing work that took me right back into the terror of psychosis and the deep intimacy I had experienced with my fiancé. I looped, in and out, through time and space, feeling and healing, understanding and releasing.

I was experiencing grief again by the time I made it to Puerto Vallarta airport. I felt ready to fly home to Glenorchy and see my son but I also felt the grief of saying goodbye to Mr. Europe, knowing that an era was drawing to an end. Knowing that we had done the big, deep work of healing the unconscious patterns that had broken us up. That we would no longer come together for two or three weeks around retreats to live and love together.

Now it was going to be all business – fly in, do the retreat, fly out.

I wept, and I wept, and I wept.

On Writing My Own Story

The context that society gives mental illness is that something is broken inside the person. That somehow they are flawed, damaged, fucked up, or rotten. And that once mental illness shows up – especially if you're diagnosed with something like bipolar disorder, or schizophrenia – that's pretty much it for life. All you can hope for is to manage it, usually through some combination of medication and counselling, and possibly wellness practices and diet.

Mental illness is seen as an aberration in the human psyche – something has gone wrong.

But not in my world.

Not in my context.

Not in my story.

Because that is all that context is... the story we choose to wrap around our experience. Usually, that story is unconsciously written based on our subconscious patterns and fears, and the social norms around us including those of family, culture and community.

But we can choose to write any story we like.

No story is true.

And all stories are true, because we make them so.

So... might as well write a story that serves to bring us into a place of wholeness, a story that serves human evolution, a story that pays homage to the essence of consciousness. Right?

And that's what I chose to do. I chose to write a story where mental illness was the doorway into greater wholeness. Where it was the gateway the soul has to pass through in order to know itself. Where it was simply a rite of passage of the evolution of consciousness in action.

In my story, I was NOT mentally ill – I had experienced an episode (or two) of psychosis.

Being something and experiencing something are two very different things.

'Being' conflates the experience with our identity.

And we tend to see and experience our identity as fixed.

'Experiencing' something makes it clear that it's a temporary thing, separate from who we are.

And that is a fucking powerful difference, right there.

In my story, I was NOT bipolar disorder – I was experiencing, in those moments, a collection of symptoms that the doctors grouped together and labelled as bipolar disorder. A classification, by the way, not a diagnosis. A diagnosis requires some kind of biological test that determines whether or not something is present. A classification looks at a grouping of symptoms and uses those symptoms to classify something – or someone.

I was experiencing a group of symptoms classified as bipolar disorder. I was NOT bipolar disorder.

Notice how this doesn't deny the reality of my experience – I didn't claim that these symptoms didn't exist, or that something didn't need to be attended to. Denying the reality of my experience – of those symptoms – would feed into the very pattern that had brought me to this place and the very pattern that I wanted to uninstall from my programming.

No, I acknowledged the reality of my experience, and the reality of the symptoms I had experienced. I listened to the doctors, I did what they told me to do, I took my medication, and I attended to my needs based on those symptoms.

But the context – the story – within which this all played out was MINE. I chose it and I created it. And this is what gave me so much power on my journey of recovery. Right from that moment in the psych ward, I took charge of myself, and my journey. And I articulated a clear strong desire as to how this was all going to play out.

'The sun is again going to shine in my life, so THERE!'

Why was I able to do this, when so many other people who experience psychosis or bipolar disorder symptoms don't?

The first major factor was that my yoga and meditation practice, and the awakening experiences, had given me an understanding of the true nature of our identity.

I didn't confuse my experience, or the 'illness', with my identity. Nor did I believe anymore that I was my thoughts, my feelings or my body. I knew myself as that which was unchanging, infinite and eternal – consciousness itself.

Likely the second major factor was my inherent rebel nature. I've always riled against the world when I could sense injustice playing out, and I've always refused to live out the expected norms. Fuck that shit. Certainly, I also used to have major people-pleaser patterning, as well as a 'tend and befriend' pattern that often overrode my rebel warrior heart. But the rebel was always there, and damned if I was going to let the outside world define me or box me in.

The third major factor that gave me the confidence to write my own story was that I'd done it all before. I'd already gone to the brink with one medical condition, wrestled control back from the system, and determined my own successful healing path. I knew that if I'd done it once, I could do it again.

* * *

Dunedin, 1991

We need to take a detour back to Dunedin in 1991– my home, at the time. I was 15 years old, and for unknown reasons, a disc in my lower back between L4 and L5 spinal bones collapsed, sending me into excruciating sciatic pain for months. Eventually, I was diagnosed with a ruptured disc and scheduled for a spinal fusion. The surgeon cut me open, sliced off some of my right hipbone, removed the collapsed disc and fused the hipbone in between the two vertebrae.

Problem solved.

But of course, it wasn't.

As per the Western medical model, I had been treated like a mechanical machine. This bit is broken – take it out and replace it. There, done. But we are not mechanical machines, and no one bothered to ask why a fit and healthy 15-year-old had a collapsed disc in the first place.

Four years later, running along a beach in Auckland during my second year at University, the sciatic pain came back. And this time I was terrified – would I need another operation again? If the first operation hadn't worked, how could the second?

For the next five or so years, until I was 25, that sciatic pain came and went. And – ever the scientist – I began to note the patterns of pain. I began to suspect that what was going on wasn't just physical but also had an emotional and mental component. Along the way I saw a handful of doctors, and I discovered they didn't know as much as I thought they did. They'd get me up on the table, and lift my leg this way and that, and test my foot for something... but all they were capable of doing was seeing what was or wasn't functioning on a mechanical level. None of them could SEE me, or what was really going on.

And what was going on got worse, and worse, and worse. By age 25 – when I was living in Whistler, about to start seeing my Australian boyfriend – the sciatic pain was chronic, daily and excruciating. My right foot began progressively getting more and more numb – nerve damage – and I started walking with a limp. Finally, I went and got X-rays done, and the verdict was dire.

Degenerative Disc Disease. And I'd need another operation.

Well fuck that.

The night I received the news – from the receptionist at the medical clinic who was a close friend – I went home, smoked my pipe, lay in bed and listened to my trance music. The prognosis played out in a spiral loop through my mind, as I sunk deeper and deeper into trance. And from that space of trance – of expanded consciousness – an intention welled up inside me.

"I'm going to heal myself."

"I AM going to heal myself."

"I am GOING TO HEAL myself."

And that was that.

I was on a mission – a journey. Something in me knew that I could do this myself. So I began, starting with Caroline Myss's book *Anatomy of the Spirit*. Next, yoga. And keen observation of everything that was going on inside me on all four levels – physical, emotional, mental and energetic. I researched, and explored, and learned, and applied.

Within six months, the chronic pain had dissipated into the occasional flare up. Within three years, the sciatic pain had gone completely and the sensation in my foot was beginning to come back. Within seven years, my foot was no longer numb. There is still a slight weakness in the right foot – a slight loss of sensation, but I am healed. My back is healed. And I have never again suffered chronic daily pain nor debilitating spasms.

That journey, already well under way by 2004, gave me the confidence to know that I didn't need to rely on the Western Medical Model to heal and recover from psychosis. Or from a classification of bipolar disorder. It gave me the confidence to know that I could take the best of what the Western Medical Model offered, and then use that information within the context of my own story – a story that felt true to me.

If I could heal myself from chronic back pain and apparent degenerative disc disease.

I could heal myself from bipolar disorder too.

* * *

There is one other factor that likely played a huge role in my recovery.

And that is that I was guided.

Divine guidance if you like.

The best divine guidance of all.

I had Kundalini herself pulsing through my veins.

Yes, it's about time I revealed more about Kundalini, because I know some of you are wondering what she's all about.

Chasing the Snake

Of course, back in 2004, I didn't know anything about Kundalini or the manner in which she would help me recover from psychosis and a classification of bipolar disorder disorder.

All I knew at that time was that the Lion's Gate Hospital doctors described my behaviour as 'bizarre' and out of touch with reality, whereas, when seen from the right perspective and with the right context, my behaviour made perfect sense.

I just needed to find that perspective, and that context.

And it was my scientist brain that got to work.

I started from the only place I could – with my memory and my journals. I knew my memory couldn't be trusted, any more than my thoughts could be trusted. But I could still go over, meticulously, every tiny single detail I could recall, and ingrain those two experiences of psychosis/awakening into my memory bank – faulty as it might be – for later use.

This meticulous examination of my experience threw up two distinct streams of happenings:

On one side, there was the metaphysical, multi-dimensional elements – like speaking in a strange language, hissing like a snake, performing kriya I'd never been taught (in this lifetime anyway), having visions, understanding complex spiritual philosophy in totality, experiencing oneness with everything, understanding that we are all merely beings of light, seeing through the illusion of material reality, and feeling grace as a living force within me.

On the other side, there were the psychological responses that patently denied reality and attempted to hold on tight to that which was gone – my fiancé. Those psychological responses could be grouped into either fear or attachment. Or both.

Seeing these two streams clearly illustrated the path that my recovery needed to take. I needed to work with my psyche to understand, heal and integrate all aspects of my shadow and unconscious. I needed to learn how to face into fear, and how to let go of attachment.

And I needed to dedicate myself to practicing and understanding yoga as a path to self-realisation.

As it turns out, self-realisation is a path that works directly with the psyche – it is all one and the same. In the yogic practices, the intention is to purify the unconsciousness in preparation for the awakening of the energy of Kundalini. But I had inadvertently unleashed the purifying, evolutionary force of Kundalini into my system before I was ready for it through a dangerous combination of mind-altering and expanding drugs, yoga and meditation, and psychological stress.

Yeah, don't take a shitload of drugs before you've done the work.

And, paradoxically, once you've done the work, the drugs will have less and less impact, as you become more centered in consciousness and less in conditioned mind.

Witness the bafflement of former Harvard lecturer and LSD pioneer Ram Dass after feeding his Guru acid and watching it have zero impact on the Guru's consciousness.

I've tested this. It's true.

You don't need the drugs. They're a dangerous short cut that can blow out your circuits.

Stick to the yoga. That's where the power lies.

* * *

On my return to New Zealand, I tried to find a yoga teacher who could help me understand what had happened, because – despite knowing nothing about Kundalini yet – I had a sense that yoga held the answers I was looking for. Class after class, and teacher after teacher disappointed me. I could tell as soon as I walked in, and the teacher started talking, whether they were 'awake' or not. Or at least, waking up. Presence has a certain kind of air about it.

And then I met Swami Shantimurti.

Queenstown, 2006

Local yoga teacher Peggy Preston had invited the Swami down from Ashram Yoga in Auckland to give a weekend workshop on chakras, or something. I signed up half-heartedly; by then I had lost all hope of finding a yoga teacher who knew anything about yoga as self-realization, or Kundalini.

Two things stand out from that experience.

On the Friday night session, we worked with Muladhara Chakra, the root chakra. Something I was in still desperate need of – grounding. This particular chakra is associated with the sense of smell. I don't recall the date that workshop was held, but I can tell you it was spring, because afterwards, walking outside, I was hit with a wall of smell. Smell in Technicolor. Smell in Dolby surround. Smell like I had never, ever known before.

I was astonished. This chakra thing was real! The association of a sense with a chakra wasn't just an intellectual thing! A bunch of yogis didn't all sit around back in the day with a list of chakras and a list of senses and decide by committee which sense went with which chakra.

'And the sense of smell goes to… Muladhara! Come on up Muladhara – you've got smell!'

No, it was an actual experiential result of working directly with that particular energetic centre in the body. Focus attention on Muladhara, do practices designed to balance and open it… And WHAM… rivers of blossom scent anyone?

That was my first taste of a workshop that felt experientially grounded in the actuality of practice, rather than simply a rote physical recitation of postures and where to place limbs.

I was eager to get back the next day to see what else would unfold. After a solid day of chakra-based practices and dialogue, what unfolded at the end of the day's session was a detailed discussion on chakras as a whole, and on Kundalini…

… ah Kundalini, she that lies symbolically coiled at the base of the spine three and a half times until awoken. She who begins to move up the spine, clearing out all physical, emotional, mental and energetic blocks before calling down the energy of Shiva from above.

Okay – it's metaphorical and symbolic. Kundalini isn't a SHE in the way you might think, but the energy of Kundalini sure as hell is feminine. And conversely, the energy of Shiva – the yang to Kundalini's yin – is all masculine. One contains and the other expresses. One is consciousness, one is energy. And together, they create everything – the entire play of the Universe.

As Swami Shantimurti spoke, he referenced different yogic practices, and how they were designed to work with specific psychological blocks in the body, and the danger of inadvertently raising Kundalini before this preparatory work had been done.

My ears pricked up. Dangers? Psychological blocks? Feminine, serpentine energy moving up the spine?

Class ended. And students gathered around the Swami to ask more questions.

I hung back, scared, emotional, in a whirl. I had to speak to him, and I was afraid to speak to him. But how could I not? I managed to force myself to get close enough to hear what was being said. The Swami looked at me – and it was that look, that presence, that sense of being seen – that which I had been craving.

This was a yogi who knew shit, and could see shit. Including, me, in all my shit right now.

My voice croaked out a question. "Is it possible... is it possible that Kundalini awakening could look like psychosis?"

There, it was out!

The swami held my gaze, with much kindness. He knew, already, why I was asking that question.

"The world's psych wards are littered with people who were not psychologically prepared for the purifying power of Kundalini when she awoke. She is not to be messed with."

And that was enough. I burst into tears, in front of the Swami, and in front of the other students. Relief flooded my whole system. A fear that I didn't even know had been gripping my heart for the past two years melted away in that springtime revelation from Swami Shantimurti.

"It happened to you, didn't it?" He asked, kindly.

I couldn't speak – too many tears – I just nodded. I wasn't crazy. I wasn't mentally ill. There wasn't something terribly wrong with me. I was okay. Or at least, as okay as someone could be when Kundalini awakens far too early.

Because while I'd always known that my experience was something spiritual, and while my rebel heart had proclaimed vehemently to the world that the sun would again shine in my life, I was still afraid, petrified, terrified, that I was crazy. That everything that had happened to me was just.... Crazy.

But finally, this Swami had validated me. Because I knew he could see me – I could see it in his eyes. And, he was kind enough to ask me to come to where he was staying for a cup of tea the next morning. There, we sat and drank tea, and he asked me questions about my experience, and then listened to me prattle on endlessly about what had happened. Finally, he gave me a few practices to do. Nothing complicated. Alternate Nostril Breathing. And chanting – om namaya shivaya. He was astute and courteous enough to ask about my home life – who I lived with and how they might feel about me chanting, before suggesting that as a practice.

* * *

Finally. Spring 2006. Two years after the implosion of my life. Now I knew for sure. Now I had a definitive context for my experience that wasn't just the story I was choosing to live out, but was a context grounded in a 5000-year-old spiritual tradition. Now there was somewhere to turn to for guidance, for support, for knowing. My local yoga teachers might not know much about Kundalini or self-realisation, but I didn't need them to follow this path.

I could find my own way.

All I had to do was let Kundalini guide me.

And practice. Practice every single day.

On Committing to Love and Truth

The biggest shift post-Kundalini is that my life became predominantly internally focused.

There was no 'out there' anymore, except as a reflection of what was occurring inside me. And so when I paid attention to 'out there' it was within the framework of knowing myself better. And with Kundalini guiding me – showing me every fear and attachment that my unconscious still contained – I couldn't hide anymore. I couldn't suppress anymore. I couldn't avoid anymore.

Or rather, I could, but I knew I was doing it... and that was a killer. A fucking killer.

Now, 13 years on, I've learned that there's no point in hiding anything, suppressing anything, or avoiding anything. If it's happening inside me, I might as well turn toward it and see what the fuck is going on.

Like this morning.

I'm perched on top of my bright orange duvet on my bed here in Laingholm, staring out the windows at the Waitakere Ranges and watching the kereru (wood pigeon) swoop from tree to tree while talking to Mr. Europe, 12,000 miles away. It's a great conversation – juicy and real – and smack bang in the middle of it he says, "I gotta go. Ivan just showed up with two beers."

Ivan is the guy in the apartment downstairs. A new friend. This is good – I'm stoked that Mr. Europe is socialising with people. He's

127

tended to be a hermit and much of his healing lies around engagement with other people.

But the abrupt way in which Mr. Europe signals he's hanging up triggers me. Massively. My belly churns. I can't speak. I'm overcome with a desire to control Mr. Europe and the situation and everything 'out there'.

"What's up? You okay?"

Mr. Europe knows, instantly, of course. Even though only a nano-second has passed and even though I haven't said anything. And, I can't hide – I want to, because it's still really, really hard for me to share my emotional reality. As if there's something weak about feeling what I'm feeling.

"I... don't feel good." I manage to get out. Tears threaten.

"I know, I can feel the emotion."

I breathe, deeply, into my belly. What the fuck? One moment I'm in a great, present space, having an awesome conversation. The next moment, I'm trigged and emotional and feel really, really shitty.

This ain't bipolar disorder. This is an old emotional trauma from childhood. This is how those traumas show up – as an out-of-context reaction to a seemingly small and insignificant exchange. When we're still mostly unconscious, these strong emotional responses are below our radar, they get stuffed down, or acted out against. We pick fights, or create dramas, and tell ourselves stories about how fucked up our partner is for ditching us in the middle of a conversation.

Not in my world. Not anymore. That trigger is felt and acknowledged for what it is – an out-of-context reaction signalling a historical trauma being re-felt. Nothing more than programming in my system – samskara, the yogis call it. Now, with our increasingly nuanced understanding of somatics and neurology, we're finally beginning to catch up with the understanding of the psyche that yogis have had for thousands of years.

It's all programming. My internal defences have been triggered because they think I'm in danger – the psychological danger of feeling painful emotions.

Mr. Europe makes sure I'm okay, and I know that he needs to go and have that beer. Even though it's emotionally killing me. And even though I know that the emotional reaction I'm having isn't about Mr. Europe, or us.

But before he goes, he offers some insight.

"It's taken you back to being a kid right? Of not feeling like you were a priority for your Dad?" That's the immediate insight and compassion that makes Mr. Europe such a good healer.

He's right. And it's something I've never been conscious of before. But as soon as he names it, realisations begin flooding through my brain. I get off the phone and turn inward, reluctantly. It's still hard to face into intense emotion by choice. And yet, the only other choice is to ignore it and go about my day as if it's not happening. But that only prolongs the misery and makes it more likely that I'll act out of that wounded space with other people in my life, creating more drama and misery.

So I do the only thing I've been able to do ever since Kundalini began to move in me. I go inward. What's going on? Why has such an innocuous comment triggered such a flood of intense emotion? What's the root of it all?

And this is the process. Kundalini brings up every single trauma, fear, insecurity, wound, ego defence and pattern to be seen, healed, released and integrated. Kundalini even seems to bring up the exact life circumstances to MAKE this happen.

The right people to trigger us, and the right jobs, the right places, the right events.

Like that toxic relationship with Mr. Toastmasters. It was toxic because I was fucked up. Because I was letting my fears run the show. Because I was acting out of wounds. Because I needed to look at my shit and heal it…

Queenstown, 2007

The day I moved into Mr. Toastmasters house – two whole weeks after our first date – I went to go to bed and his four-year-old daughter was sleeping in our bed.

Now, I'd grown up in a family where there was never ANY co-sleeping. It wasn't something I was familiar with at all, and it freaked me the fuck out. And, it also triggered a childhood trauma. The same one that's triggered right now – the feeling of not being a priority. Because when I pointed out that his daughter was in our bed, and I wanted to go to bed, he just said, "Move her over, she won't wake up."

But I wanted her out of our bed. And I started having all kinds of intense emotional reactions including a feeling of total dread in my belly.

What had I just done? I'd just moved in with this guy after two weeks! And only six weeks after breaking up with my last partner. That fear and dread built up in my stomach and had become visceral by the time he came to bed, and moved his daughter back to her bed. We lay in bed, next to each other, first night in the house together as live-in boyfriend and girlfriend... and we were marinating in fear. Both of us.

And then we both saw something black and shadowy scamper up the wall behind us and through the roof.

What the fuck was that?

"You brought a demon into this house!" he accused me.

A demon? I replayed what I'd just seen – black, shadowy, scampery... a demon? How could this be happening? But he saw it too. He named it before I did.

I shook my head frantically. "Maybe it was leaving? Maybe it's been released?"

I still don't know what it was that we felt and saw that August evening, but it didn't surprise me. And as I fell asleep, full of dread and fear, there was part of me that knew I had to play out this relationship, whatever this was, however this felt. I had to ride the wave till it reached what shore awaits. Even though it felt like it was going to crash, and crash hard. Still, even with that sense of knowing, I had to ride it.

Sometimes shit just has to play out.

And so ride it out I did. For three and a half years. As I struggled to understand the dynamic between Mr. Toastmasters, and myself I turned it into my own psychological training programme. I used every conflict between us – and there was weekly conflict – as a way of knowing myself better. Seeing myself more clearly. Understanding better who I was.

This desire to know myself and heal myself was the filter that Kundalini had placed over my life – it was all I cared about. Knowing myself and clearing out all the crap.

Because while the relationship was toxic as all hell, Mr. Toastmasters was also incredibly intuitive and insightful. And not shy about throwing all my fears and insecurities in my face. Some might call that verbally abusive. Hell, it WAS verbally abusive. But I allowed it, and I used it. I used his nasty insights as a reflective mirror. Because while he was sometimes mean about what he saw, he did see true. He saw when I was crippled by fear, and it was repulsive to him, and he let me know. And so I began to notice from the inside out when fear was gripping my heart and guiding my actions.

And, I could see – feel – that his frustrations and anger came out of his own wounds and his own pain. I understood him, and because of my patterning around co-dependence and care-taking, I resolved to love him into wellness too.

He called me controlling, all the time, which I didn't understand for the longest time. But slowly, I began to see and understand that when I was scared – which was a lot of the time – I'd do everything I could to control myself and control him and control the situation. The entire relationship felt like I was walking on eggshells – I never knew what might set him off. And yet, this experience revealed my major pattern of being in the world, and specifically of being in relationship.

The reason I felt like I was walking on eggshells was because I constantly looked for external cues on how to be and how to act as a method of feeling safe and loved. It never occurred to me, nor did I even know HOW, to just 'be me'. This pointed to a deep belief that if I WAS me, I would not be loved. That in order to be loved, I had to be what was required of me.

This set up an unconscious dynamic where I had an expectation that if I was the 'perfect girlfriend' according to the needs and desires of my partner, then he would play the 'perfect boyfriend' according to my needs and desires.

Of course, my ex didn't have this script. He didn't know that this was my unconscious expectation. And when he didn't play it out, I constantly freaked out, which confused him all to hell.

We were fucked up, playing out all our unconscious wounds on each other. All the while loving each other deeply.

Messy, so fucking messy.

But I made it through. Because I was practicing yoga, reading extensively, and writing myself awake.

* * *

Wellington, 2009

One significant breakthrough.

I'm in the kitchen of our Wellington house, the house Mr. Toastmaster and I are renovating, and the house whose mortgage I'm paying through my job as a speechwriter for the Ministry of Social Development. He's angry at me, for something. He's going off on me, like he always does. It's verbal abuse. All of a sudden, out of nowhere, I hear myself say, "You can't talk to me like that. I won't have it. You can't talk to me like that, not anymore."

I watch him stop. A startled look comes over his face... and he turns away.

And that's it. He never verbally abuses me again.

He was as unconscious as I was. And somehow, the work I was doing, and the learning I was doing, and my ability to finally name and energetically hold a clear boundary, shifted something in the dynamic between us.

That's how I justified being in that relationship for so long – even though I tried to leave seven times. I knew I was growing. I knew I was getting my shit together. I knew I was becoming a better person. I knew that I was using the relationship as a way to wake up. And of course, I loved him deeply, because he was an extraordinary man – wounded and beautiful.

* * *

132

Dunedin, 2010

The turning point came when I went to LA in 2010 to complete my yoga teacher training with Shiva Rea, global prana vinyasa teacher, activist, and innovator in the evolution of vinyasa yoga. She was an ashtangi yogi until she started to have visions of the Mother during her practice, and her body started to spontaneously move in ways that were most definitely not in the strict ashtanga sequence. My kind of teacher.

That teacher training gave me ten days out of our relationship. Ten days of yoga all day, every day. Ten days of being around people whom I didn't trigger, and who didn't trigger me.

I felt like I'd come out of a hostage situation, and through the lens of comparison I was finally able to feel how damn toxic and messed up our relationship truly was, despite the positive growth.

On the return flight to New Zealand I made a vow to myself. Because I knew it was all about me. It wasn't about him at all. That's something that Kundalini makes patently clear. Nothing out there exists, except as a projection or a mirror. If this relationship was going to shift and change, it would come from how I shifted and changed.

So I made a resolution. I was going to be completely loving and accepting of my partner as he was. And I was going to speak the truth in every moment. No more wanting him to change, no more wanting him to be different, no more wanting him to love me in a different way.

No, I was just going to love him as he was. And then be truthful in the moment.

That was it.

No big deal right?

Truth and love.

The cornerstones of any decent relationship.

* * *

Like this morning. Me, here in Laingholm in 2017, sitting on my bed talking to Mr. Europe. Me, managing to choke out that I'm triggered and feeling intense emotion. And Mr. Europe, being able to hear and hold me in that truth, with love.

A simple exchange with no drama, no stories, and no bullshit. Just vulnerability and truth of one's experience.

It's taken me years of hard work to get to this point – to be able to share my emotional truth with someone I love. And it's still fucking hard. I'm still hitting up against a wall of fear and emotion every time I have to speak up. But I keep speaking up.

And that resolution I made, flying home to Dunedin from LA in 2010, that was the beginning of the shift. The beginning of the commitment. The beginning of real, authentic, loving relationships.

First though, I had to allow the natural ending of the toxic mess I'd been in for three and a half years. I had to let go, and stop trying to make it into something it wasn't. Stop trying to make my partner into something he wasn't.

I had to accept him.

Love him.

And speak the truth to him.

I'd left this relationship seven times and I always ended up getting sucked back into the sticky dynamic of unconscious patterns. Because I loved him. Because he loved me. Because the good times were great. Because I was afraid of being by myself.

But once truth was made sovereign, nothing else mattered. I stopped shutting up and started speaking up, and the amount of conflict between us accelerated as everything once hidden suddenly got laid on the table. And I finally saw the truth. This man's wounds were not mine to heal. And he wasn't particularly interested in healing them himself. He was not my problem. I was my problem. I could love him, and choose to not be with him. The two were not mutually exclusive. This was about what was best for me, and best for the beautiful baby boy we'd chosen to have together. This was about what I wanted to experience in day to day living for myself, and for our son.

So I stood up and said, 'enough. I'm done.'

And finally, I was.

Two months, that's how long it took, from committing to truth to final ending.

Two months.

The Resurgence of Kundalini

This is the path of Kundalini. Truth. And facing into the sticky situations that show you where you're stuck, where you're not aligned, and where you need to wake up.

After I left Mr. Toastmasters, in late December 2010, I had a surge in Kundalini symptoms. She'd always been active in me, in small subtle ways, since 2000. Any time I stopped still – say on my yoga mat – and began to breathe with total awareness, my body would begin to spontaneously move through a yoga practice. It felt like a force within me seeking out the areas of tension and stuck-ness within my body and pouring warm liquid into them.

This would also happen at night. I'd lie down to sleep, become aware of my breathing, and feel Kundalini moving within me – mostly in my spine. She'd move up my spine until she hit a blockage, then there would be a small popping sound, the blockage would dissipate, and she'd fall back down again to the base of my spine. Until she moved up again, and possibly hit the same blockage, and the same sensation would occur, and she would drop back down again.

When I first became aware of this process in my body, back in the winter of 2000/2001, when I was living in Whistler with my Australian boyfriend, the sensation of rising only made it up into my lumbar spine.

Now, after almost two decades of this process, the sensation of rising and releasing is mostly focused around my neck and skull.

After leaving Mr. Toastmasters, that sensation became stronger and more powerful – hotter and more electric. I was exhausted from running after a one-year-old all day, by myself, and I'd drop into bed, so ready to sleep. And then Kundalini would start to rise, and rise, and rise. I would find myself wired as all hell, lying awake for hours, Kundalini doing her thing. Sometimes she'd move me into yoga postures, right there in bed, and I'd suddenly be doing Bridge pose, or even Wheel pose.

It disturbed my sleep but also brought comfort. The resurgence of Kundalini energy in my body felt like a confirmation that I was on the right path.

* * *

Wellington, 2008

I'd felt that striking confirmation of the path before – one other time when I'd almost left Mr. Toastmaster. It was after we'd just bought that house in Wellington with his deposit and my salary. The plan was that I would pay the mortgage on my speechwriting salary while he renovated it. We were moving out of our damp, dark one-bedroom apartment in Newtown and into the new – but very old and rundown – house. His family were coming to help us move and so I'd made a big pot of chicken soup to feed everyone. I'd made the soup because I thought it would make him happy – he always talked about the kitchen being the heart of the home, and about hospitality. And he'd always been disparaging about my cooking skills.

In my script, making the soup would both feed everyone, and make him happy. And then he would shower me with love and affection and I would get what I needed/wanted.

That didn't happen.

He didn't give a shit about the soup.

And instead got angry with me over the phone from the new house as I made soup in our old apartment.

I got off the phone and was bereft. I found myself on my hands and knees sobbing out buckets of tears. I didn't know how to make this man happy so the loving side of him could come out. I felt completely powerless and lost and alone and trapped. That began a descent into darkness for me, compounded by the shift into the new house. I just couldn't get it together, I couldn't stop crying, and I felt totally lost.

In the end, my Dad told me to come over for a few days to his place in Blenheim, a three-hour ferry ride across the Cook Strait. It was a welcome respite from the trauma of my relationship with Mr. Toastmasters. I could feel myself again and think straight. It became clear to me that I had to get out of this damn relationship – that it wasn't healthy. I was sitting in my Dad's conservatory, all big windows and garden outside, when I made this decision. And as I said it out loud – 'I'm done, I'm leaving, it's over', I felt and saw the room get brighter. Like a cohort of angels had filled up the room.

It was extraordinary.

I was on the right path.

I knew it.

I could feel it.

Follow the light, right? Well there it was – light. Confirmation of the path.

I headed back to Wellington, taking the ferry and then splurging on a taxi, feeling connected and so powerful. This was MY life and I was taking control.

Then I walked into our house, and into his presence. And everything – all of it – went out the window. Neither of us said a word... I was just sucked back into the matrix of our relationship. Light... gone. Hello darkness, welcome back.

* * *

Dunedin, 2010

Two years later I did a cord-cutting session with a healer on Mr. Toastmasters. It happened during that window of time between my commitment to truth and the final leaving. The healer gasped, loudly, when she went in to scan the energetic connection between the two of us.

"When people are in a romantic relationship together, they have a unified bubble of 'togetherness.'" she explained. "For most people, this extends about 12 feet out from their body. But the two of you..." There was a sharp sucking intake of breath. "The two of you... are fully merged... as one being... all the way out... into... deep space."

One being.

That explained... everything.

It explained why I felt like I wasn't myself, why I was constantly being sucked into his world and his life and his views and his perspective. Why, when I would be by myself, I would get clear and feel my truth, and then as soon as I was back in a space with him... it all disappeared. Like that time coming back from my Dad's place. I knew, standing in the conservatory feeling and watching the light grow all around me, that leaving was the path. But I literally could not act on it when I returned home to Wellington.

So maybe it wasn't just the commitment to truth that helped me finally leave that relationship. Maybe the cord cutting and energetic clearing played a role.

Because one month later, on the night I left – the night I stood up and said "I don't want to live this experience anymore." I had the same experience as in Blenheim.

* * *

Glenorchy, 2010

I was standing in my Mum's lounge in Glenorchy; we'd driven there for the Christmas holidays, with plans of camping in a caravan in the backyard. Standing out there, I told Mr. Toastmaster I was done. That I'd be sleeping in the house with our one-year-old son and that I was done. I was leaving.

Afterwards I stood in my Mum's lounge and felt everything get light and bright again – a sensation that persisted over the next few days and was so strong that even my mother commented on it. She could feel it and see it too.

Finally, I had guided myself back on track, back into the light. So when I took our son a few weeks later and moved up to Wellington – Paekakariki, where a generous friend offered us a room, rent-free – so that Sam could be close enough for his Dad to see him regularly, I wasn't surprised to find Kundalini starting to surge more dramatically each night in bed. I didn't mind too much, even with the lack of sleep, because it seemed like validation that I was doing the right thing, taking the right steps. That there was something bigger than myself out there – in here – that I could trust.

Follow the light. Who knew that it could be so damn literal?

That was the last relationship I had that focused on me trying to be someone in order to get something. That had been my pattern – the one that had caused so much suffering. And I was done. No more trying to control a relationship, or a man, in order to get what I wanted. Another pattern that had caused so much pain.

Instead, I'd finally discovered the courage to start living my life from truth, as best I could, trusting that one day, love would also show up. Because that was one of my biggest fears – that if I was myself, just as I am, I wasn't loveable. That to be loved, I had to watch for all the subtle signals and signs of what was needed, desired and accepted and respond to that.

Total external orientation.

A survival mechanism.

And one learned in childhood.

If I behave the way you want me to, I will receive your love and I will be safe.

My parents didn't mean to programme me that way.

But they did.

And this was the result.

When I got into relationships, I reverted from 'being me' to being whoever I perceived was required to gain love. And then, if that strategy didn't work and love was denied to me, I felt powerless and unsafe which then triggered emotionality and a controlling aspect. Neither of which are very attractive. It was a self-defeating spiral.

My fiancé fell in love with my natural self – who I was. And then, as we fell deeper in love, my programming activated and I tried to be who I thought he wanted me to be... Which pushed him away... Which made me feel powerless and unsafe... Which triggered emotionality and control... Which further repulsed him. And then completely panicked me because my biggest fear – that I was fundamentally unlovable – was being proven true.

Here was this man who loved me, and yet as he got to know me more, he began to un-love me.

Panic.

Suppression.

Panic.

Suppression.

Awakening breaking the ability to suppress.

Panic.

Hello psychosis – panic plus a strategic mind on a hyper-loop desperately attempting to control things and make them the way I thought I needed them to be so I could feel safe and loved.

Because that's the thing once Kundalini awakens. None of the old psychological strategies work anymore. Or, they begin to slowly erode and break down and reveal themselves for the false structures that they are. Every strategy I had developed as a child to feel safe, to find and keep love, to feel worthwhile, to navigate the world... all of it was destined to break apart once Kundalini started to move.

In an ideal world, the systematic practice of yoga would have ALREADY dismantled these patterns in a gentle, loving and supported manner. This is how human evolution is meant to happen. But I didn't have a teacher guiding me, nor had I done enough prep work, and my ego structure was heavily defended and patterned.

As Swami Shantimurti had explained, the world's psych wards are littered with people like me – people who awaken Kundalini before they have done adequate preparation work to stabilise the psyche. And, without context, nor right relationship to the unfolding evolutionary force of Kundalini, there is no way to skilfully and meaningfully work with what's showing up.

Because what's showing up can be confusing as all hell.

Life as My Lover

Laingholm, 2017

Kundalini is strong in me right now.

It's difficult to write – to type even. She's moving through my neck and throat – jutting my chin forward, lifting my gaze skyward, rolling my eyes right back in my head. A snake, seeking liberation, winding and wending it's way up my spine, along the nadis and out the crown chakra.

I can stop her – by shifting out of total surrendered presence and into the doing aspect of Self. But it's fucking tough right now. Even as I type, my eyes are still rolling back into my head and that makes it hard to see what I'm writing. Thankfully, I'm an expert touch typist.

Sometimes I go into Kundalini trance and video myself, just to see what it looks like. What is going on? It looks pretty fucking crazy even to me – it's like I'm possessed sometimes, cycling through different characters and archetypes. From rigid body movements to flowing body movements to rapid jerking, from tears to laughter.

* * *

In my medical records from 2004, the doctors note that my fiancé described me as rapidly cycling through shifting emotional moods – laughing one moment and crying the next. Definitely crazy right? Yet only a few months ago, sitting in practice in my bedroom in Glenorchy, I was very much sane and had exactly the same experience.

One moment, I was deep in a profound realisation on the nature of play and the absurdity of so much of what we perceive as real – dissolving in a fit of laughter and joy and bliss. Then, while understanding the role a particular girlfriend has played in my life, I was hit with waves of teary gratitude. All the while witnessing myself having these experiences.

From bliss and joy.

To tears of gratitude.

And back again.

Within a heartbeat.

In 2004, with no context and no dedicated, daily yoga practice, it all seemed insanity. In 2017, with both context and dedicated, daily yoga practice, it's the unwinding of my psyche and the unfolding evolutionary process of being human. Suggesting, as some psychologists say, that psychosis is the psyche attempting to heal itself. (Check out the work of Paris Williams for more on that.)

Right now, the pull to sit in meditation for long periods of time is strong. Every time I stop in my daily life – stop working, stop driving, stop talking – I drop into trance state. It even happened at the garage today in Glen Eden, as I waited for the mechanic to finish servicing my van.

The increase in Kundalini energy is most noticeable at night usually, when I close my eyes to sleep. With nothing to distract my attention, and all of my awareness on my breath and my body, Kundalini begins to move instantly. And as soon as she does, I go from being weary to being alert. I've learned to keep my eyes closed though, and focus on softening my body and slowing my breath. Usually, I'll fall asleep within half an hour after some pretty intense energetic flows. No wheel pose in bed these days though! Not like I was experiencing in Paekakariki back in early 2011!

Right now, it feels like she wants me. I paused for a moment there, to take a breath and see what to write next. The moment my hands stopped tapping on the keyboard, I found myself in a two-handed mudra, gaze again focused on the flickering candle on my altar, a remnant of my yoga practice before sitting down to write.

Another indicator that I'm about to enter a Kundalini phase – I don't want to eat. Oh, I feel hunger, but every time I walk into the kitchen to make myself some food, I'm drawn to only a light snack. Eating heavy and dense food slows Kundalini down while fasting speeds her up. I always get a sense of not wanting to pollute my body at all, of only wanting clean food. Yet I'm also aware of a need for balance and grounding. Lack of food and sleep can take one deeper into trance states, but it can also take one into mania. My choice of lunch was a roasted vegetable salad at a local cafe up in Titirangi. It took me almost 90 minutes to eat – one slow mouthful at a time, but I knew that nourishment and grounding was key so I persisted, even though it felt like Kundalini didn't want me to.

It sounds like I'm talking about some parasitic entity that's taken over my body, but Kundalini is not like that. It's more like being held by the Mother of all Creation. Like the Goddess herself is loving you from the inside out. Indeed, it can feel very much like the entire world is making love to you, which makes for some very interesting experiences.

* * *

Taupō, 2016

Like this one time, on my way to Wanderlust Great Lake Taupō, with a close friend – stunningly talented photographer Pete Longworth. Our plan was to stop at Kerosene Creek and do a photo shoot before rocking up to the four-day yoga and music festival. Pete and I had become fast and intimate friends during the previous Wanderlust when we stayed up all night – literally – on a midnight mission to some local hot springs, and then enjoyed a drawn-out talkfest.

Pete's the best photographer I know, so I was honoured, excited and freaking nervous about doing a photo shoot with him.

Turned out to be the best photo shoot of my life.

Like me, Pete is all about the flow and sensual pleasure, and so as the sunset and light beams cut through the forest, we cranked the tunes on my cherished Bluetooth speaker. That created a soundscape of DEEP & SEXY vibes from DJ Alex Cruz – music I'd listened to hundreds and hundreds of time alone in my bedroom, dancing, yoga-ing and playing. The combination of nature plus somatic music memory began the process of dropping me into the deepest trance I'd experienced since 2004. Only this time, someone who loved me and accepted me completely was witnessing me. Someone who understood intuitively where I was and what I was going through.

The music played as the sun bathed the forest in late afternoon light and I began to practice, like I do when no one is watching. Practicing just in the clothes I'm wearing – a dress and yoga pants, No yoga mat – and relating intimately with the natural world around me. I used trees, and rocks, and slopes, and grass to support and extend and release my body.

All the while, Pete is radiating love and joy from behind the camera lens, dancing around me, clicking and angling and delighting in everything I'm doing.

This goes on for what feels like hours – so long that night has fallen by the time we're almost finished. And we finish shooting in the hot pools themselves, steam rising from the waterfall behind me. But even before it gets to this stage, I'm deep in the throes of love making from the inside out. I've dropped so deep into trance and am feeling so connected with the earth and the sky and the light and the water and the flow... that I feel like the world itself is making love to me.

The water helps to ground me, washing away some of the excess energy that has built up over the duration of the photo shoot.

Finally, we're done, and Pete takes a selfie of the two of us as we exit the water, scramble into clothes, and hit the road in my trusty Ford Laser to make the final dash to Wanderlust.

I'm buzzing all over.

Like really buzzing.

Buzzing like you do right before you...

"Holy fuck!"

I'm driving, and I'm doing everything I can to focus on driving, bringing my bestest yogic skills to focus and attention. Lights on, speed limit obeyed, eyes on the road...

But even then... it happens...

I begin to have an energetic body orgasm. "Holy fuck!"

Pete glances over. "You okay?"

I can't help myself... I can't talk either, as the energetic goodness continues to roll on through my body and it takes all available bandwidth to stay focused on driving. Safety first! Finally, I'm able to get a word out and glance sideways at him.

"Wow." I say, pausing for dramatic effect, knowing just how much Pete is going to appreciate this. "You know... you're the first man to give me a full body orgasm... without even laying a finger on me."

Pete's eyes bulge out of his head, he slaps his thighs. "HOLY fuck! I did wonder what the hell was going on just then..."

I shake my head. Technically, it wasn't really Pete that gave me that orgasm (or five), it was Kundalini herself. It was the trance state of flow that I dropped into when those magical ingredients of music, yoga, movement and nature under the loving and appreciative eye of a man all came together.

I'd had some extraordinary sexual experiences in my life – particularly with my fiancé – but this topped everything. Never before had I had such intense orgasms just from the very play of life pulsing through my veins.

It was a welcome portent of things to come though...

Sex on the Astral Plane

Nighttime. Laingholm, 2017

My legs are slippery with coconut oil, post-bath, and so I've propped my laptop up on a pillow so it doesn't slide down my legs.

I'm still sitting on my sheepskin rug, candle still lit in my altar, from doing Day 600 of my practice.

Six hundred days.

Feels like a milestone worth celebrating.

Six hundred days of turning up and doing the same Tantra Hatha practice no matter what.

Today, somehow, I broke up with Mr. Europe, for the second time. Or at least, acknowledged the truth that was becoming more and more apparent to me.

I love him. Our connection is deep and strong and intimate and powerful. We work astonishingly well together.

And yet, I don't want to live the life that would ensue if we were to live a life together. It's not just the 12,000 miles that separate us. The essence of how we operate in the world is different, and I no longer want to be in the space he occupies.

Painful.

Fucking painful.

He's here in three weeks, obstinately so we can see if we do 'belong' together. So in a way, we had never come back together since I left him in May. But the intent was there… to explore and see if it would work now that he knows he only wants to be with me. And yet it seems I already know. I can already feel it.

147

And to complicate matters, I've been feeling the presence of another man. Deeply. Strongly. Pulling me.

I don't know who this man is – although there are a few possibilities floating through my being. And I don't know if this man I've been feeling is a real man, or an archetype of a particular kind of man, or a delusion of the mind – my own doubts finding a way to wriggle out of real intimacy with Mr. Europe.

Actually. I do know. That's what today has all been about – dropping into, feeling, and naming out loud that knowing.

This man I can feel is an archetype of a man, rather than an actual, particular man. But somehow, his presence on the astral level has made clear the truth that's been tugging at my consciousness for the last four weeks or so, since Mr. Europe booked his ticket to come and see me.

We are not romantic partners, Mr. Europe and I.

I know this. I feel this. And I need to own it.

I need to own it despite my fear that I won't meet a man who I can be as real and true and intimate with as I am with Mr. Europe.

Because that's the thing with Kundalini, with Awakening. It's impossible to live from fear anymore. Fucking impossible. It just becomes so painful, and so clear, and so obvious anytime I make any choice that is fear-based.

Like stepping back into relating with Mr. Europe.

Fear-based.

I was afraid of being alone, afraid that there wouldn't be another man as nuanced as Mr. Europe is in dealing with the subtleties of life. Someone as motivated to face down fear and show up to truth.

So I leaned into Mr. Europe as he reached out to me and then there we were, him coming to New Zealand, me organising a bunch of events to pay for it all, and us getting back together.

Only now we're not.

* * *

The first time Mr. Europe and I had sex, it was of the astral variety and I didn't know it was him.

Mt. Maunganui, 2016

148

I was in my kitchen in Mt Maunganui, where Sam and I lived for 18 months before heading down south to Glenorchy. Mr. Europe was (obstinately) asleep in the lounge, where he'd been crashing since arriving a few days previously from Croatia to lead a Retreat with me in Taupō.

We'd been friends online since 2014 – both writers for *Elephant Journal*, both deep into spirituality, both Leos, both attracted as hell to each other and keeping mum about it. I'd interviewed him for my website *The Yoga Lunchbox*, and after his marriage broke up, we'd started Skyping each other on an irregular basis. He'd done a few private healing sessions for me, and they were bloody powerful. So, with a lot of respect for him as a healer and an interest in him as a man, when I learned he was looking to do more retreats I invited him to New Zealand.

Eight months later, he's asleep in my lounge, and I'm in the kitchen waiting for the jug to boil and doing yoga. Nothing fancy, just a standard forward bend with my arms out-stretched and hands on the bench in front of me. I was playing with releasing my hips and spine, which tend to be tight.

This involved lifting my heels off the ground, bending my knees, tilting my pelvis as far forward as I could to create space in my hip joints, which does mean that my arse is right up in the air at a very convenient height, but with only the stove behind me, sex was the last thing on my mind.

The jug had likely boiled by now, but I was deep into my practice and had begun to move into a more fluid flow, shifting my hips in a circular direction and from side to side.

Then, suddenly, there IS a man behind me, one hand on each hip, drawing me in and up toward him and sliding his...

What the fuck?

I can't help but look behind me but no one's there. Of course no one's there – it's just me and the stove and the fridge and the now-boiled jug.

Curious, I drop back down into the posture and into my breath and begin to surrender again into sahaja – the spontaneous flow of movement. Into Kundalini.

149

And BAM. Wham... there's that sense again of a man being behind me, holding me, guiding me... this time, I stay with it just to see what's going on... and I could swear, someone is making love to me as I yoga it up in the kitchen. I daren't go all the way so I break the connection, make my cup of tea, and disappear back into my bedroom.

* * *

It was only later, after Mr. Europe and I did have sex (which happened for the first time the day after the retreat finished) that I realised it had been Mr. Europe with me in the kitchen. I knew it was him, because when we ended up like that in bed one night and I recognised the way he was holding me, guiding me...

Much later, when I'd got up the courage to share my astral experiences with Mr. Europe, I asked him about that night. What he'd been doing in the lounge. If he remembered it. He didn't. Or so he said. But who knows...

Because it wasn't the last time Mr. Europe came to me on the astral plane. In fact, during that year we were together, especially when I was still living in Mount Maunganui and taking regular baths, it happened often – maybe every week. It felt like dropping into an alternative reality, and I guess in many ways it was. Most people don't feel the energetic realms the way I do – as if they are completely real and material. But to me, they are. They exist. And they contain all kinds of information and energy.

Once, I was even visited by a different man. I thought it was Mr. Europe at first – of course! – but as soon as we began to move together, I knew it wasn't him – he had a completely different energy and approach. Initially I went along with it out of curiosity, and because I know this man in real life also... and then I broke it with a start. Was this cheating on Mr. Europe? Was I committing astral infidelity?

Of course, eventually I told Mr. Europe about that experience and that man, because Mr. Europe and I operate on total transparency.

***

Laingholm, 2017

Which is why the last four weeks have been so incredibly challenging and confusing for me.

On one hand, I finally had the thing I'd wanted – Mr. Europe was fully committing to me and whole-heartedly wanting me. No more open relationship for him – he wanted sacred monogamy too, after more than a year of doubt.

And yet... even while I organised events to finance the trip, so Mr. Europe could come and see me, there was this other man consistently showing up to hang out with me on the astral plane. Another man who possibly existed in real life, but I didn't know who he was. I just knew what he felt like.

It seemed a Faustian choice, between the real man – Mr. Europe, here and whole, committing and loving – And this other astral man –not here with me, not offering anything, yet embodying a quality of masculinity that was calling to my heart in a way that Mr. Europe did not.

I meditated on it. I journaled on it. I contemplated and had baths and walked. And in the end, I went with the real man who I loved deeply and who was showing up for me in a powerful way.

It seemed right.

It seemed clear.

And yet... I still felt torn. Even as Mr. Europe stepped up in a way he never had with me, declaring his committed love for me, organising his own visa and booking his own tickets.

I loved Mr. Europe. This much I knew was true.

I had to go with that.

So I let go of the other possible man.

* * *

Laingholm, 2017

As I've touched on before, living with Kundalini sometimes feels like living in Hell or living in Heaven, because the heightened states of

151

awareness that come with Kundalini make it so clear where I'm living from. When I'm in alignment with heart and presence and All that Is – everything is in a state of flow and I feel connected and alive. When I'm clinging to something, or living from fear, I experience intense emotions, and often old traumas come up to be healed. Which means life can feel very sticky and difficult.

It's as if She shines a spotlight on those places where I still need to trust, surrender and let go. And when that fails, she whips my arse. And when that fails, she rubs salt in the wound. And when that fails... well, it doesn't really. I've become more and more attuned to the subtle guidance of life whispering in my ear. I don't want to be whipped anymore, I don't want salt rubbed in my wounds. And I definitely don't want my life to implode again!

Stepping back into potentiality with Mr. Europe shone a light on the attachments and fears that I was still entertaining.

This didn't feel good.

I turned inward to face what wasn't feeling good. I did the work on clearing the places I was attached and the places I was still afraid.

And as I did this I began to sense, to feel, hell, to KNOW that I couldn't wholeheartedly embrace a life with Mr. Europe. It wasn't what I wanted. It felt like sacrificing myself. Like it wasn't my life.

I wanted it to be. Oh, how I wanted it to be...

But it wasn't. I was operating from a space of being afraid to hurt Mr. Europe, afraid of losing him, afraid of not connecting with another man the way I connect to Mr. Europe... I was operating from fear.

And because Mr. Europe and I put truth and love at the centre of all our relating, I couldn't hide any of what was going on for me from him. That would be betraying truth, and the moment you betray truth, you've lost the connection.

So I had to lay it all out for him. And in naming it – my doubts and fears and pull towards this other man on the astral plane – in naming it, the truth became clear to both of us.

I didn't want to be with Mr. Europe.

"I can't blame you," he said. There was a long pause.

And my heart bled. "Can you feel how much I love you?" I said.

"Yes." Long pause. "Thank God."

Because that's the thing.

We do love each other.

But love is not enough. Love is not all. Love is not the path. Love is the field we swim in when we let go of fear and fully open up to another person. It's not dependent on two particular people finding each other among 7 billion. Love can exist between all and everyone.

It's the other stuff that defines whether or not a life is meant to be built together. The sexual attraction. That begins to narrow down the field. Compatibility. Shared life mission. That's the biggie – shared life mission. Mr. Europe and I come so close on this one. We share a similar mission. But our approach is different, our way of engaging with the world and in the world is different. And to be with Mr. Europe would mean I'd cut off an important part of how I want to play and express in the world.

I can't do that.

Not anymore.

That's one childhood pattern that I said goodbye to today, forever.

No more shutting myself down for fear of not being loved.

I want to play, and I want to play HARD.

On Facing the Fears

Last night, again, she came. When I finally closed my eyes at 11:30pm after holding Mr. Europe on the phone while he grieved our transitioning relationship (I was so damn tired!) there she was. Kundalini. Pulsing through my veins and up my spine and preventing me from falling asleep for almost an hour. Moving, writhing, seething, pulsing.

So active right now.

It was okay though. I didn't need to get up in the morning.

It was my childfree last morning before my son came back from his Dad's.

But still, I was wide awake at 7am. Wide awake and tired.

There was a voice message from Mr. Europe.

"Thank you for really being there for me, it really helped me a lot. Most of all feeling the love you have for me. Really helped with the feeling of rejection. Even though we're not going to be together romantically I want to maintain and keep the intimacy and the connection that we have. I want to know what's going on for you... even when it's a bit painful for me. It feels important to me that we don't step backwards in terms of our communication and the intimacy."

Bam.

My biggest fears – of hurting Mr. Europe, and losing Mr. Europe – dissipated in one voice message. Because I was honest about what I was experiencing and continued to love him deeply through it all.

It was painful, last night, sitting on the phone and listening to him sobbing gut-wrenching tears because I didn't want to be with him

155

romantically. I listened, and I held him energetically, and I was right there with him.

And he owned his feelings, completely. With no anger, and no blame. Just being with what he was feeling, completely.

It takes an extraordinary man to do that. And it's part of the awakening process. To know and feel and see that everything you feel is all about you. To know that the greatest power of all lies in owning one's feelings completely.

Mostly, we do everything we can to arrange our lives to guarantee nothing but comfortable feelings. We choose to be with people who make us feel good, and get angry with them when they break the contract and trigger uncomfortable feelings inside us.

Awakening turns that inside out.

It did for me.

I began to see that nobody could make me feel anything that wasn't already inside me. I began to see that the people and circumstances of my life were only there to wake me up.

Even this situation with Mr. Europe.

Which has remarkable parallels to my relationship with Mr. Toastmasters.

Another man I loved so deeply.

Another man I had to screw up the courage to finally say no to because I knew I didn't want to live out the experience of being with him. Because I wanted a different kind of life – I wanted my life.

This is what happens. We encounter the same pattern, the same feelings, the same spiral... until we finally heal the underlying pattern or release the underlying fear. It's all a giant game really, a video game. A reality game. Just don't start looking for Fear Factor flags that aren't there.

Somewhere deep inside, I had a belief that I needed to compromise myself in order to experience love. And so, I kept ending up in relationships that asked that of me, and then caused all kinds of suffering. Beliefs create reality. Until they don't.

This morning, when I woke up too damn early at 7am, I felt light – light-hearted, light-spirited, and light in body. The heaviness that had plagued me for the past four weeks or so was just... gone. This is what it feels like to face down a fear – to know what you're afraid of, look it straight in the eye, and take the action that risks that reality.

I was scared of hurting Mr. Europe.

And I did hurt him. Or at least, he experienced intense emotional pain because of my actions. But because I stayed with him – connected, open and loving – he also experienced being held in unconditional love while feeling great pain. And love always, always, always trumps pain.

I was scared of losing Mr. Europe.

Instead, he's asked me to stay intimately connected with him on a soul level, even while we no longer seek to create a life together nor are physically intimate.

I feel like I've risked all... and gained everything.

Sure, I'm single again. Back there, without a man by my side, without a man to create a life with... and yet even that doesn't seem to matter so much anymore. It doesn't seem to matter because there's plenty of connection, intimacy and love in my life. All that's missing is the sex... yet even that... if I tune in deep enough to Kundalini – especially while out in nature, or dancing – I can feel life itself making love to me. The world becomes my beloved, and I its lover.

Do I yearn for physical love?

Yes and no. I adore the pleasures of the flesh, and could spend days in bed with my lover, rising only for food, showers and cups of tea. But my state of being is more and more grounded in the here and now. There is no sense of yearning for that which is not present. And when there is a yearning, or a sense of lack, it only points to the place where the work is still to be done. It points to the next step in my evolution. In my en-light-enment.

Because that is all en-light-enment is really. The unshackling of one's being from the conditioning of mind and society. The dissolving, releasing and healing of fears. The unconscious becoming conscious, made so by constantly identifying and moving towards fears.

⅄ ✳ ✳

One of my greatest fears was motherhood. Specifically, single motherhood. And you know what life dished up?

Yep, single motherhood.

It felt like I'd finally done enough work to escape from the pain, suffering and confusion of my toxic relationship with my son's father... but then I had to face into the challenge of being a single mother of a one-year-old child with no income. On the benefit.

Challenge upon challenge upon challenge upon challenge.

Escaping to an ashram under the guidance of a Guru would have been so much easier. But life didn't dish that up to me. Instead, post-awakening experience, I was forced to do all the hard work of awakening while navigating an ordinary, householder life. I went from a toxic relationship into single parenthood, all the while starting up a business and attempting to face into my mental and emotional challenges.

Without a guru to guide me, I had to rely on my own discernment. Dodgy, when your mind already has a rap for betraying you. Yet that was the best thing that could ever have happened to me because it showed me that the mind was not to be believed. Ever. How could I know whether a thought was a deluded thought, or a wise thought? What was the difference?

Because there is a difference.

And when you study your thoughts for long enough, under a powerful enough microscope, you do begin to discern the difference between thoughts of the Mind, and thoughts of Knowingness. I experience Knowingness as more of a felt sense, and thoughts more as concepts and words. Knowingness seems to come from the lower half of my torso, and thoughts from above the heart. Both have their value, but only one can be trusted implicitly.

Which is why the last four or five weeks were so challenging. I could sense the truth of what was going on with Mr. Europe, but my fears got in the way of truly knowing and being able to articulate it. That's what fear does — it shuts us down. It spins all kinds of fancy stories about why we should take the job, or shouldn't take the job. Should stay in the marriage or shouldn't stay in the marriage. Should buy that plane ticket or shouldn't buy that plane ticket. Fear argues and wheedles and rationalises and justifies. Truth just is. No debate.

Yet it's only now – 13 years on – that I'm really getting clarity on why life has been so fucking tough for me since the psychosis.

It's fear.

That's all.

Every time I lived from fear, made choices based in fear, let fear guide my way... I suffered. And when I suffered, I turned inwards and did everything I could to find the source of my suffering – which was often beliefs or childhood ego defences or behaviour patterns. Then I'd identify whatever it was and uninstall the programme. Doing that meant I would release some of the fear, and life would get better for a while.

But fear still lived inside me, driving me forward. And so invariably, I would drop down again into depression, into suffering, into misery.

It's been a long, hard, fucking painful road. Yet I kept showing up. Kept doing the work. Kept going inward. Trusting that eventually, somehow, I would find that place of bliss and contentment that I experienced in Whistler before the psychosis. That place of flow and ease where magic happened.

That place where fear doesn't live.

Now, I feel like I might have just faced into my biggest fear of all.

That of losing the love of a man I love deeply, by living from truth.

* * *

Fuck.

Flashbacks.

To my first relationship, where I thought I lost my boyfriend from living from truth but really, lost him because I lived from indulgence and temptation and pleasure.

To my third relationship, where I was too afraid to live from truth and so when the crunch between truth and boyfriend become too tight a squeeze... instead of daring to trust my boyfriend and speak my truth... I broke up with him first.

To my fourth relationship, the one that led to the psych ward, the ultimate example of what happened when I couldn't speak up, couldn't be true and couldn't let go.

And so the wheel turns, over and over and over again. Until the original pattern is healed and we no longer need to play out the same drama anymore.

The original pattern that has caused all this heartache over the past two decades?

That came from my relationship with my Dad.

The first Man I ever fell in love with.

On Fear of Intimacy

t's all intertwined, of course.

My relationships with men, founded on the beliefs and fears I developed through my relationship with my Father.

My father, doing the best he could, within the constraints and understandings he had of parenthood, unwittingly setting me up with one of the biggest fears of all.

The fear that I would not be loved if I spoke up and was myself.

Leading to a belief that the only way to receive love from men was to be who was required. Who was needed.

That led to a way of operating in relationship that was completely externally focused. I was always looking for the cues that revealed who I needed to be so I could hold on to love from whichever man I was with.

This is the moment to drop in that perfect anecdote that would illustrate the installation of this pattern. But when I search my childhood memory banks using the keyword 'father', scant entries fill the page.

There's my father, taking us fishing beside lakes and streams and rivers and oceans. He fishes, we play – climbing trees, making damns, swimming, and sometimes fishing.

There's my father, scooping me up off the grass after I stood on two bees at once and holding me in his arms as he dashes me up to the house.

There's my father, holding court in our faded brown Lazyboy chair, regaling my brother, sister and I with fishing stories, including his favourite: the lifecycle of the salmon. We're clustered around the bottom of his chair, gazing upward at this tall, handsome, articulate man, whose way with words has us wide-eyed as the salmon swims back up the river to spawn – even though we've heard it all before.

That elusive memory to explain my programming just isn't there. Which suggests that it wasn't one particular incident. That instead, it was a subtle, insistent, daily way of relating – that of the authoritarian parent – that shaped my relationship to men. Do what you're told, or else. I heard that a lot growing up. And I was afraid of my Dad – afraid of upsetting him, afraid of his anger, afraid of not being who he wanted me to be... because I just wanted him to see me and love me. And I didn't feel that. He was too lost in his own torment, going through his own private hell.

During those formative years – from about 4 years until 12 years – my Dad was suffering. He didn't have anything to give to his children. The blackness took him, and it took him all the way to Ashburn Clinic where he too was diagnosed with bipolar disorder, and given Lithium. I was old enough then – 11 years old, to see what the Lithium did to my Dad. There was no more holding court in the Lazyboy and regaling us with stories of the salmon's life cycle. My Dad was fighting for his own mental survival.

A year later, my parents divorced and my mind rationalised it as a good thing, because Dad was too harsh to live with anyway. Twelve years old, and I had already developed a strong emotional survival defense mechanism. I held it all in, and down, and out of my awareness.

Fear – of feeling the truth.

Fear – of feeling the pain.

Fear – of what was going to happen now.

Fears.

They've completely ruled my life.

Unconsciously, of course.

Which was okay until the awakening of Kundalini in 2004. Before then, I could live from fear, and not suffer – consciously – too much.

But then I experienced a window of time where I was outside of fear and immersed in total bliss and oneness. And when I came crash-bang-smack into my flawed and human self again, unconsciously living from fear was no longer an option.

Yet it was all I knew how to do.

I was petrified – of everything.

162

And landing back in Glenorchy, New Zealand in October 2004, I was still unaware of those fears that were running my life, even as they continued to propel me forward. I flew to Auckland in November because I was afraid of being a failure and so was determined to succeed. I wasn't chasing success through my innate creative contributions to life, but instead chasing it desperately, almost haphazardly, in order to prove that I wasn't a failure, which was a massive fear.

When applying for media jobs failed, and the precarious state of my emotional and mental state sent me fleeing back down south – first to my grandparents and then to Queenstown – I started churning out writing. A memoir, of sorts. Articles. I pitched a TV show. I submitted the memoir to a national competition. I submitted articles to national publications. Not because the work had merit – although some of it did – but because I needed something or someone – anything or anyone – to prove that I wasn't a failure.

Which is what I felt like.

That fear of failure drove me for 12 years. Unconsciously. It was the fuel that saw me create my first blog, *Be Conscious Now*, in 2006, and my second one, *The Yoga Lunchbox*, in 2008. "See me! Validate me!" I cried out from every article, every social media post, and every interaction.

All the while, wondering why I felt unseen, unvalidated, and like a massive failure.

It wasn't until I came back to Glenorchy, in February 2017, that I was able to finally make conscious that unconscious fear of failure.

There's something about returning to the physical location where a fear is first felt, or created, that gives it an opportunity to come into consciousness.

This sabbatical to Glenorchy came off the back of six weeks in Croatia with Mr. Europe. It had been an intense, deep dive immersion into all my neediness and insecurity as a woman in relationship. Mr. Europe hadn't reacted to any of my shit, and with immeasurable skill had held space for all my craziness to come out. And I, in return, had owned all my projections and fears and freaked out behaviour, determined to do the work on it so I could relax into romantic relationship without disintegrating into a total mess.

Because disintegrate I did. Why? Fear – abject fear. I was terrified of not being loved for who I was, terrified of being a controlling bitch, terrified of all the strong emotions and sensations that got triggered when I loved someone. Because that was the thing – loving someone terrified me. I discovered that the very thing I craved most – deep intimacy – was the thing I was most afraid of.

Flashback to Mr. Europe's house.

Croatia December 19, 2016

This morning... I woke up and went straight into a triggered space. I saw everything through the perspective of, 'he's doing this or not doing this and therefore not the right person for me.' This way of seeing created a super strong sensation of wanting to run. I battled the mind shenanigans around this all morning. I felt fucking terrible. So terrible. And on top of that, I began distancing myself from Mr. Europe – pulling away and withdrawing. And I could feel all of this happening.

So now I'm miserable and I end up sobbing in the bathroom upstairs. He's in the upstairs office, working. I walk out of the bathroom. He calls me into the office. Fuck. I can't avoid it. I go in.

"What's going on?"

I don't want to say anything. I don't want to share. I'm afraid. I can watch all this inside my mind and body, unable to speak.

He asks me again. I'm looking at him. Silent. Knowing what this says. Knowing I have to speak, that it's the only way. I can't not talk – that's not an option. Avoidance. And if I speak, only truth can come out because I'll know instantly if it's anything else. And so will he.

I begin to talk. It's haphazard. I edge around things. Mr. Europe asks direct – "Is it Samuel? Is it me? What is it? Why are you upset?"

I fudge. "I'm not sure, possibly... maybe..." But I know that as I talk, the truth will come out. It always does now. Especially if I'm speaking to someone who can also smell bullshit with the nose of a sommelier. I'm trapped. Nowhere to go. And nowhere to hide. I have no choice but to speak the truth.

Somehow it comes out – that I feel like he's been absent today. Here in physical form but not in presence. And I don't want to experience that. I don't want to be with someone physically and intimately if they're not actually with me. I begin to lay out all the evidence that supports my belief that this is how he is being – you did this, and this, and this. All these things – you did them, and that means THIS.

He looks at me. And then tells me what he thinks. That Samuel is the more important thing right now – and I'm making it all about our relationship, or all about how I'm feeling.

I listen. He's right. I can hear it. I also feel like I'm in the Principal's Office being reprimanded. Reprimanded for not being fucking perfect all the time.

Yet I also hear what he's saying.

He stops talking. Looks away. I look at him, and say nothing. He continues to look away and then begins to scroll through Facebook again. Obviously I'm done and can go now, so I leave.

I'm tearful still, and I stop at the top of the stairs. I don't want to go down crying. Not with Samuel there. So I walk forward into the bedroom and round the corner to the sunrise window. There's a crystal hanging in that window, one I brought with me from New Zealand. One I've owned since Whistler. It's been in every home I've ever lived in, usually in my bedroom window, usually facing east.

I stand under that crystal and look out the window and feel into my body. I stand with my arms on my hips and I feel the truth of my experience. I feel what was true and right and what needed to be heard. And then, hands on hips. I walk back into Mr. Europe's study.

"There's two things here," I say.

"One is that I do need to focus on Samuel. And the other is it feels like you absented yourself and that triggered me. Those are two separate things, but both can be true and happening."

Mr. Europe looks at me, and with patience goes through each example of when I said he'd been absent that day, explaining how there were valid reasons for his behaviour in each instant.

I look at him, hearing his truth, a cog shifting in my mind as my experience and his experience open up reality in front of me.

"I know, you're right," I say.

He starts to explain again and I stop him.

"I believe you," I say. "My projections weren't real at all – it was just how I felt. And that's what was going on. I was feeling these things based on a belief that wasn't real. And it was freaking me out."

Everything shifts in that moment. No longer are we arguing about what happened, but instead understanding the two very different ways each of us experienced the same event. Mr. Europe holds me. Tight. Whispers in my ear. "You're amazing. You're doing great work. I love you."

Later, much later, I realise the fear that had been triggered. My Dad was mostly emotionally absent. He'd be in the house, but he wasn't there. He was never there. And then he left for good.

That was the fear that got triggered.

That was the childhood trauma.

All the heartache I'd felt when my Dad disappeared emotionally when I was a child.

* * **

That's an example of one small moment of the time in Croatia where I was crippled by fear originating in childhood emotional trauma. I was hyper-conscious of any kind of checking-out by Mr. Europe – learned behaviour from childhood. So any time a man I was with appeared to checkout – take space – it would trigger this deep fear of not being loved and I would get hyper-emotional and lose the plot.

My projected idea of reality created real emotion in me and triggered massive drama in my past relationships because the men I was with couldn't see what was actually going on any more than I could, so they couldn't hold me in that space of emotionality.

That entire six weeks in Croatia, I wanted to run like hell. But I couldn't. I was in a foreign country and didn't know the language and had nowhere to go. So I was stuck, and forced to feel whatever came up. Which turned out to be my deepest relationship wounds, which in turn increased the desire to run. The stronger the desire to run, the deeper the wound. I was so fucking scared to let go and be in love with Mr. Europe because I was so scared of losing him.

Fear again. Ruling me. But I knew it. And I knew then that either I fully let go and love him completely even though he could be gone tomorrow, next week, next month, next decade, next lifetime...

...Or I could hedge my bets and try and protect myself by bringing out all the defences to protect my heart. Those defences of the heart – the desire to keep ourselves emotionally safe from pain – were exactly what stopped me from being ME in every relationship I had ever had. I was scared of not being loved, scared of being left, scared of loving someone, scared of intimacy, scared of FEELING.

So my entire relationship with Mr. Europe became about identifying each defence and seeing it for what it was... before completely disarming it and continuing to grow inwards, towards opening my heart completely to the experience.

True intimacy.

A path for heart warriors, willing to shine a light on one's own shadows.

A path where the relating itself – truth and love – is the most important thing, rather than the form of the relating. Which is why this week, back home in Laingholm 2017, breaking up with Mr. Europe again, felt like the final and biggest test of all. Because I could feel that I was back in a place of fear, and that was keeping me stuck and silent.

I was afraid to tell Mr. Europe that I could sense our path was not one of creating a life together. It didn't mean I didn't love him. It didn't mean I didn't want to continue to be emotionally and spiritual intimate with him. It just meant fronting up to the truth.

He lives in Croatia with his young son. My path is in New Zealand. And I didn't want to experience the kind of life that we would need to have in order to be together.

Telling him the truth was scary as all hell.

But I can't not speak truth.

Reality demands it of me.

Kundalini demands it of me.

Life demands it of me.

And now I demand it of myself... No more fear.

On Being Afraid of the Teacher

Laingholm, 2017

know now why Kundalini was moving so strong in me this last week as I felt into the truth of Mr. Europe and I. Or at least... I can put forward a hypothesis.

She was calling me back into truth, into alignment.

Just as she seems to increase in strength and energy when I realign – like after leaving my son's father – so too does she gather strength when she wants to get my attention.

I feel her now, as soon as I drop down into being-ness. That place where time ceases, where thought ceases, where all sense of being a separate being begins to fade away. What wonders would await me if I were alone in a cave overlooking a forest with nothing to do but meditate and practice?

Life would be much simpler, and easier. I imagine I could commune with All that Is and never truly come up against my own fears and beliefs and insecurities and doubts and issues. Or rather, daily practice – for hours – would do the heavy lifting for me, and slowly but surely dissolve away all the samskaras, all the karma, and all the crap that I'm lugging around with me.

Instead, stuck smack bang in the middle of a householder life, my entire existence turns into one drawn out sadhana where every interaction with another person becomes a way for me to know myself – see myself – and do the hard work of unwinding my samskaras and karma.

All without a teacher. Which means I've probably taken the hard road – got stuck in mud where I could have stepped on to a light rail and whizzed over that section.

Even in this, I'm stuck. I don't trust teachers or gurus and I'm afraid to be seen by a teacher or guru. It's a double bind, and one I've only become aware of in the last year or so.

Post-psychosis, I was eager to find a teacher who could light my way. Yet after that one interaction with Swami Shantimurti, I never sought him out again. And even when we were in the same place at the same time, I found myself unconsciously avoiding him.

Embarrassment, possibly. At who I had been in 2006 when he'd first met me. Fear, likely, of what he would see now. And perhaps also fear that with all the work and awakening I've now done, that I would see his humanness. Which could lead me to doubt his view of me back in 2006.

I did find a teacher I could work with physically, once. Peter Sanson, an Ashtanga teacher who'd spent serious time with Ashtanga Guru Pattabois Jois, in Mysore, going for three months every year for two decades. Peter saw the energetics and emotional blocks that were stopping my physical practice from progressing, and so in January 2015 I moved across the country to work with him. Left Glenorchy – the second time I'd lived there – took my four-year old son and moved to Napier.

There, I went two or three times a week to an old stone building in the middle of town with worn-through carpet and stained glass windows, and I practiced Ashtanga. Peter presided over the room with one or two assistants as up to 40 people went through the exact same sequence, every time they showed up. It was valuable for me, useful, to have that kind of strong container to practice in. There's no escaping anything in Ashtanga. The sequence is as the sequence is, and it intelligently and systematically opens the body up.

Under Peter's watchful eye, I dropped all kinds of tensions and had many insights. Yet I was also profoundly aware of the shortcomings of the sequence – the narrowness of the scope. And it felt to me like Peter was stuck in a role, not waking up, just being where he was – a skilled and insightful teacher of asana. In all likelihood, I'm wrong on this. Yet that is what it felt like to me at the time.

So I took what I could, and when I left Napier for Wellington, and then Mount Maunganui, I continued to find a Mysore-style Ashtanga studio. Then I got to one particular posture that was impossible for me to do because of the range of movement in my wrists. I'd hit bone compression – something that Ashtanga denies is real. The party line states that dedicated yoga practice can change bones. And frankly, that pissed me off. I wasn't interested in pouring myself into a physical yoga practice so I could change my bone structure. I wanted to wake up. And I recognised that practicing asana was one way to clear blockages out of the nadis and so release samskaras.

Yet I also knew that yoga practice itself was often co-opted by Maya – by illusion. That adherence to a system was the very thing that Kundalini breaks through. That believing in a set sequence for everyone, no matter what, is bullshit. And besides, where the fuck where all the awakened Ashtangis? Because when I looked around the room – when I felt the energy of the room – what I sensed was a bunch of people reinforcing the structures of their ego through the systematic practice of a sequence likely designed for young teenage Indian boys.

It was all bullshit.

I tried to stick it out – attempted to modify the posture much to the consternation of my teacher. Argued with him about it. Asked to go on to the next posture. But in Ashtanga, you don't 'progress' until you master the former posture. There's much wisdom in this – when applied within context and through a particular relationship – but if it becomes just another arbitrary rule, it's Maya in action.

So I ditched the Ashtanga. Maybe I'll drop into one of Peter's classes if we're ever both in the same town – he's a damn fine teacher and he has the sight. So much can be gained. But I wanted more.

No teacher has showed up since then, although I've trialled a few. At Wanderlust 2017, Rod Stryker was teaching. He'd been on my radar for a few years because his foundation is Tantra Yoga and I've been looking for a teacher to learn direct from. So I was stoked when Rod showed up at our local festival. I made it to two of his classes –

one mostly asana, and one Yoga Nidra. He impressed me. I liked the approach he took to asana – the focus on the breath, the simplicity, and the repeated movements. And Yoga Nidra has long been one of my favourite practices.

Yet when I went to his Speakeasy, I found myself getting frustrated. The topic was that of his book – *The Four Desires: Creating a Life of Purpose, Happiness, Prosperity and Freedom*. The focus was on the material world – succeeding in that world. I wasn't interested in chasing imaginary temptations of Maya. I wanted to know about waking up. So I cornered him after class, and asked what was possibly an insulting question. I was trying to figure out where he was coming from – what his motivation was. Why was he writing about happiness and succeeding in the material world? Wasn't that all just illusion anyway? Was it some smart and sneaky marketing technique to hook people on the Happiness before spoon-feeding them awakening?

Yes, I think I may have said that – suggesting that his approach was about slick marketing.

Rod responded to my ineptness with grace, and I'm paraphrasing. He said something about how before you can focus on waking up, you have to master living in the material world. Otherwise, all kinds of shit can go wrong. And most people were still at the stage of needing to master the material world.

Now, maybe he was bullshitting me. Maybe it was all about marketing and being a successful yoga teacher. But whatever it was, I avoided him for the rest of the Festival. I was afraid to go up and have a conversation with him. I had a sense that he would be able to see right through me. Or something. Maybe I was afraid that the only way for me to engage with him would have been to probe and argue and debate to try and find out what was true, and I was afraid to do that.

Whatever it was, I was in avoidance. And I noticed that.

Ah the dilemmas of finding a teacher in the 21st century. Made all the more difficult because it's now become commonplace for teachers to fall from grace – we've even got an article on *The Yoga Lunchbox* which lists out the different scandals various yoga and spiritual teachers have become embroiled in, starting with Bikram Choudbury, perhaps the one yogi that even non-yoga people can name.

I saw him once, on stage, giving a lecture. Bikram Yoga was a consistent part of my studio practice for years – it was accessible to my tight body in a way that Ashtanga never was. In fact, it was only after consistently practicing Bikram Yoga for about ten years that I was finally able to access and move into the floor postures of Ashtanga. Before that, my hamstrings, pelvis and spine were far too tight. So on a physical level, Bikram was a powerful practice for me.

And, interestingly enough, it was also a powerful practice on an emotional and mental level. Practicing 26 postures twice over in 40-degree heat forces you to totally surrender. You simply cannot stay in the room if you insist on fighting and resisting the heat. And my entire ego structure until I was in my mid to late twenties, was based on resisting, fighting and fleeing life. I had no idea what it was to surrender to anything. I was shit scared – unconsciously – of surrendering. So Bikram Yoga had a powerful psychological impact on me. It began the process of unwinding the defence patterns that were on high alert 24/7. And I needed that – I've always needed ways to access letting go and surrendering because my controlling aspects were so strong for so long.

Whistler, 2002

I was living in Whistler, Canada when I first started Bikram Yoga. The studio was down in Function Junction, an arts and industrial zone just a ten-minute bus ride from my apartment in Whistler Creek, the original ski area. In winter, the 40-degree heat was delicious. I would melt my way through class, shower, and then bus back to the Creek, before walking five minutes through head-high snowdrifts back to my apartment where I would collapse on to the couch, unable to move for the rest of the evening. Bikram completely wiped me out, for at least the first few years.

And then I began to burst into tears in the middle of class – generally when we got to Dancer's Pose, which was a standing posture about 30 minutes into the sequence. On a really bad day, I would sniffle and silently snob for the rest of class. This was the un-doing process – years of unfelt emotions and unfelt tears were beginning to surface.

Of course, I was also still partying like a rock star, even while going to yoga. Saturday night I might hit Sushi Village with my Australian boyfriend, drink a few litres of sake, sober up with a few lines of coke, hit the dance floor at Tommy Africa's with a Black Russian or two, chased with a few more lines before staggering home for coked-up sex.

Monday, I'd make it to the studio, and sweat it all out in practice.

No wonder I couldn't move after class.

My dedication to Bikram Yoga continued whenever there was a studio in my town. Showing up to the same sequence, the same heat, and the same process felt good when everything else in my life was constantly changing. It meant that I could see and know myself through the consistency of the practice. I could feel a progression – not just physically, but also emotionally and mentally. Those first few years, just staying in the room was a challenge. But eventually, the heat didn't touch me and I never thought of leaving again.

Auckland, 2012

Post-awakening, I was still dedicated to Bikram Yoga as a practice when I heard that Bikram himself was coming to New Zealand and delivering one lecture. I happened to be visiting family in Tauranga when he was going to be in Auckland – Mission on. I left Sam with my Mum, hopped in the car, and drove three hours to sit in a lecture room and watch Bikram strut up and down on stage like a peacock while delivering a well-practiced and well-worn patter of ego bullshit.

I wasn't surprised. But I was disappointed. I wanted to know if he was awake at all – even just a little bit. After all, he'd been practising his own sequence for decades, and if the practice of asana was meant to wake you up, surely he'd be proof?

He was proof – proof that asana alone has nothing to do with waking up, and that most yoga students have no idea that their teachers are sometimes full of bullshit.

The guy was asleep. He was so asleep, that when he took questions towards the end of the lecture, he wasn't able to be present enough to listen to what the person was asking and respond. You know, basic communication skills. Instead, no matter what was asked, he found someway to twist the answer back around to deliver one of his marketing spiels.

He was a bullshit artist. And he had the entire Bikram world under his spell. That I could see, plain as day. Although I didn't know the extent to which his spell had deceived people, nor the misery it would cause when it all came to light in a few years' time.

I left disillusioned.

Where were the awakened Masters? Did any even exist? Who the hell did you go to see if you wanted to Wake Up? Was waking up even a thing, or was it all just bullshit?

And so it was back to just me, by myself, on my mat, with Kundalini guiding the way.

Projections and Mirrors

In the yogic traditions, the term 'Kundalini Awakening' is not what happened to me. A 'true' Kundalini Awakening is when Kundalini stirs from her resting place coiled three and a half times around at the base of the spine and shoots clear up the Sushumna channel and exits the crown of the head.

Nothing blocks her way. She gets stuck precisely no-where. And she doesn't get shunted into either of the other two nadis – Ida and Pingala – that wend their way caduceus-like up the spine.

No, a true Kundalini Awakening is a homerun all the way from the base of the spine to the Crown of the head and beyond. And then, Kundalini descends again, coming back down and, bringing Shiva with her this time, into the heart of the aspirant, where the Mother and Father of the Universe – Shiva and Shakti – birth a new consciousness.

The ancient yogic texts are full of warnings about the dangers of awakening Kundalini before the clearing of the channels has been properly done. All kinds of neuroses and psychological problems can ensue.

Maybe a more accurate term for my experience would be Kundalini Stirring. Or Kundalini On-the-Move. But really, she's awakened, and so the term Kundalini Awakening has come to mean any kind of experience where Kundalini wakes up and begins to move.

Historically, there's a bunch of people (who may or may not have existed) who also experienced awakening of Kundalini. People like Jesus Christ. And Joan of Arc. And pretty much any of the other Christian mystics you want to name. Also, Muhammad. And a handful of the other prophets from the Islam tradition. One of the side benefits of Kundalini is the potential to activate all kinds of super powers – like the power to heal, and the ability to see into the future. Or to know the future.

Tick and tick.

But those super powers – called siddhis in the yogic traditions – are not the real deal. And in fact, they can become obstacles on the path because they're so damn alluring that one can become enthralled by the power they offer and forget about going all the way to self-realisation.

Which is what I suspect happened to so many of the fallen gurus along the way.

Kundalini awakened. She started moving. Siddhis started to appear. Followers started to gather. Power started to accrue. And then all the shadow aspects – all the unconsciousness not yet dealt with – also started to power up. Because that's what happens. When you get more powerful, ALL of you gets more powerful, including your shadow side.

And the thing with being the dude up front sitting on the podium telling it like it is... all the followers project all their unconscious shit on to you, and their projections prevent them from seeing you clearly. As do their desires. For so many of us, the desire for a saviour is so present and so strong; it overrides our ability to see what's what.

Add to that the fact that in the West, those attracted to spirituality tend to be the most wounded, abused, suffering and fucked up of us all, and you have a recipe for disaster. Because if the material world is working just fine for you – great job, great house, great car, and great partner – why would you want to look at the unseen world?

Maybe Mr. Bikram did experience a degree of opening and awakening. Certainly he was a skilled asana teacher. But without anyone to call his bullshit and help him deal with his shadows as they came up... perhaps he became more and more mired in Maya – in illusion. Whatever we don't own inside of us gets projected outside of us.

Like this…

* * *

Laingholm, 2017

Yesterday, my iPhone 6 died, again, on 38% battery. It's not even four years old yet and I've already replaced the battery once. But it seems it's determined to give up the ghost on me, forcing me to buy yet another handset when I would be content to use the same old hardware for the next five years. It's only recently updated to OS 11.02 or something... and I swear, part of me wonders if they deliberately insert code into those updates to suck your battery life so you must buy the newest shiniest product from them.

Yep, off the back of my iPhone dying, again, my mind was spinning all kinds of conspiracy theories, and ranting about built-in product obsolescence even as I was surfing my phone company website to see what a new handset would cost me.

Knock knock knock!

Someone was at the door. Unusual. People rarely just show up on doorsteps anymore. I open the door.

'Hi, is Ally here please?'

It's a clean cut, professional man, with a hint of hipster cool, about my age.

"Ally? Illy? Do you mean Illy?" I live with another single mum and her daughter Ileana.

"No, Ally."

"There's no Ally here."

This goes on for a few more exchanges before I finally grasp that Ally is his daughter and a friend of Illy's and he was meant to pick her up from here as Ally and Illy are on a playdate. Illy and her mum aren't back yet from Illy's play date – which means neither is Ally, so I invite him in to wait.

We sit down on the couch and he asks me how I am. I skip the social niceties, and answer his question honestly, watching myself with curiosity as I launch straight into a dialogue about how I'm pissed off. Pissed off because I feel like I'm being forced to buy a new phone thanks to deliberate built in obsolescence. See, this is the thing about allowing life to flow through me – a'la Kundalini – I never know quite what's going to come out of my mouth. Yet I'm learning to trust it, more and more and more. Even when it doesn't fit social conversations. And now, I'm curious to see where this is going to go.

"Huh," he says. He's somewhat taken back by how forthright I am, but cool enough to drop into the groove straight away. "I work in product development actually, it's one of the things we work with."

What? Of course he does. Here's me, deep in mind chatter about the nature of product development in our capitalist world, and Maya sends in a guy who works in product development to talk to me.

Because, after about ten minutes of detailed and illuminating conversation on the nature of product development and obsolescence, almost as if he was reading from a script that said 'now exit stage left', the man sits up straight and says, "Oh! I think I'm meant to pick Ally up from Illy's *Dad's* house! I'm going to go and check my phone – it's in the car."

And he's out the door. And whaddaya know... he was meant to get Ally from her Dad's house. So off he goes, back into his world, after making a surprise entrance into mine to deliver detailed information on the evolution of product lifecycle development. Information that reassured me that other people are making sure that product development evolves in a way that supports our limited resources.

* * *

My takeaway? Product lifecycle development is not my business. Kundalini's got other people taking care of that, and there's going to a big shift in the way we work with materials. It's already happening, and I just got a peek into that world. I can just let it all go.

If I need a new phone, I need a new phone. My rant about being forced to get one is just me resisting reality. And anytime I resist reality, I'm not trusting my own ability to navigate reality. Author Yogananda's *Autobiography of a Yogi* lays it all out, clean and clear:

"My guru, awake in God, knew this world was nothing more than the objectivised dream of the Creator. Because he was completely aware of his unity with the Divine Dreamer, Lahiri Mahasaya could materialise or dematerialise or make any other change he wished in the dream atoms of the phenomenal world."

For good measure, Yogananda includes a quote from that other great text, *The Bible*.

"What things soever ye desire, when ye pray, believe that ye receive them and ye shall have them." Mark 11:24

Sounds like a manifester's wet dream right? Anything you want! Just create out of thin air!

But it doesn't work like that. Because what's created out there is always a reflection of what you contain within you, and most people contain all kinds of unconscious shit and shadows and darkness. Plus, so many of us are still ping ponging between seeking pleasure and avoiding pain, between attraction and aversion – I want that. I don't want this. But Waking up is about letting go of it all, and surrendering to the flow of Shakti within. Surrendering to the play of the Universe.

Waking up is waking up to that flow of evolutionary energy within and simply aligning to it... surrendering to it... allowing it to be what it is. Understanding that there is a cause and effect for everything, and sometimes, shit's just got to play out because that's the karma.

Then, the universe does become like a giant playground where all your needs are met. Notice I say needs, not wants. That's a key distinction.

That phrase I just quoted from *Autobiography of a Yogi*? In the middle of writing the paragraph above it, I remembered that Yogananda shares many stories about the bending of reality. The book is on the shelf behind me. I pick up the book, and take a moment, asking for a passage that will skilfully demonstrate my point. And then I open the book to page 113 and at the very top, there was that quote. Exactly what I needed.

Mere coincidence right? Total luck?

Maybe. Maybe indeed. I don't know. I'm not too attached to any ideas of what it might be... I just notice the smoothness of my intention and what showed up.

That lack of attachment is crucial. Because I have nothing to prove. Whether or not you believe me is completely immaterial. In fact, I would be delighted if you didn't believe me. Please don't believe a single thing I say! Because all belief is a construct. Instead, be like a scientist. Test it out for yourself. Start to play with material reality as if it were a giant, malleable dream world, and you are dreaming it all up based upon your unconscious beliefs and ideas of what the world is like.

And, start to use the world out there as a giant mirror, reflecting back to you all the unseen aspects of your Self. If you keep coming up against the same type of person – a bully for example, ask yourself; 'What the fuck is going on here?' Get real curious about what the bully might be able to teach you and show you, how they might be able to shine a mirror on an unseen part of yourself ready to dissolve.

Where is the bully inside you?

Are you a people pleaser who needs to learn to stand up for himself?

How does the bully make you feel?

What's your habitual response to the bully?

Do you turn into a victim?

Do you suppress your anger?

Do you make excuses for the bully's behaviour?

In short, how does your dream character interact with that dream character in the Matrix of our world? And how would you LIKE to interact with that dream character? Who would you choose to be, if you could choose to be anyone? And why not? Why can't you be like that?

Because that's not who you are?

But who are you, really?

Underneath it all... all the behaviour patterns, learned in childhood as a way of getting love and as a way of keeping safe... all the fears... all the insecurities... all the masks... all the roles... all the identities... who are you? When you dive right into yourself, and peel back all those layers, and see what lies underneath...

What do you find?

* * *

Welcome to Yoga.

Welcome to Waking Up.

Welcome to Self-Realisation.

Because maybe... underneath it all... you're nobody at all... or conversely... you're everybody.

What then huh?

What then?

Dreaming of Hanumanasana

Laingholm, 2017

Last night I dreamt of effortlessly opening into Hanumanasana, a yoga posture named for the Monkey God, Hanuman.

I was on the shores of an expansive lake in a large underground cavern with sun shafting down through holes high in the ceiling. People I knew came and went – relationships of varying significance. And in one moment I find myself lying on my back on the hard rock, practicing yoga. I'm astounded to discover that I can lie flat and lift one leg up into the sky and draw it all the way back towards my shoulder until it lies flat along the side of my torso.

Hanumanasana. The splits, but upside down.

I'm astonished and delighted.

Such ease... wow!

Then I'm sitting on the ground, upright, and I slide one leg forward and one leg back. Again, total ease and my legs are completely flat.

There it is.

Hanumanasana.

So named for the great leap that the Monkey God, Hanuman, made when he went to rescue Sita from the evil Demon King Ravana. A leap from the tip of India all the way to Sri Lanka. Nothing could stand in the way of Hanuman – he was the ultimate action hero, and completely dedicated to his Lord, Rama.

It could be said that Hanuman embodies the phrase, 'where there's a will, there's a way.'

In real life, there is no ease in my splits, just as there is no ease in my forward bends. Sometimes I still feel as stuck as I ever was in postures, although this is not true.

I often dream though, of melting into postures like this. And it always feels extraordinary. So this is what it's like to fully surrender into a forward bend? Into the splits?

There were sexual undertones to last night's dream as well. Pete, that close friend and talented photographer of mine, was scouting the cavern with me so we could shoot powerful photos – not enough light, was his verdict.

Then I had a sense of waiting for a man, of knowing that a particular man was going to join me down there and we would swim together. He didn't show – but another of my good male friends did.

After that, when I found myself in the splits, I was joking with my photographer friend about the benefits of being that limber now.

The cavern reminds me of svadisthana – second chakra. The sacral chakra. That which rules relationship and intimacy and pleasure and our sexuality.

The gift of this chakra is our ability to feel and sense our way through life – something that was denied to me for about the first 40 years of my life. I had a complete shut down on the feeling side until at least 29 years of age. Oh... I was capable of sexual pleasure and feeling... but to emotionally feel and sense my way through life?

In total denial.

I'm edging around the outskirts right now of sexuality. I know I have to dive into it, that it can't be ignored, that it is a large element of my story and of awakening in general. Yet, I notice myself hesitating – do I want to go there?

Guilt, shame, fear. These are the three demons of the lower three chakras – of muladhara, svadisthana and manipura. Together, they keep us all tied up in knots and unable to effortlessly ascend into our heart chakra – into anahata. There, the demon is grief. And it was that grief that was my entry point back into the world of feeling and sensing.

Grief over the loss of my relationship with my fiancé.

184

Grief over the loss of my entire social network in Whistler – over the loss of my Tribe.

Grief over leaving a town and land I loved.

Grief over the loss of my life as I knew it.

But also the grief that remained unexpressed and unfelt from the previous 29 years – of the break-up of my family and the feeling that I was losing my Dad, of seeing my mother in total fear about providing well for my siblings and myself.

Oceans and oceans and oceans of grief.

In the lead up to, and during, the awakening/psychosis experiences I felt total love and oneness for everything. It felt like my heart chakra had blasted wide open. Perhaps that is what happened, and in the blasting open of that energy centre, all the stored and unexplored feelings were finally liberated.

Then, post-psychosis, everything shut back down again and the pain was excruciating. Living from an open-hearted space compared to living from a closed-hearted space is, as I've shared before, like the difference between Heaven and Hell. Now that I knew there was another way to experience life – a heart-open way that didn't require the assistance of MDMA to attain – I was committed to doing everything it took to find my way back in there.

Hanumanasana. I was going to rescue myself from the prison of my closed heart, no matter what it took.

Tears now, as the truth of that hits me. Tears, at the realisation of how I have rescued myself, that I have been committed to my own evolution in the same way Hanuman was committed to rescuing Sita from the clutches of Ravana. For I have cried glaciers worth of tears in the last thirteen years. At first those tears were violent retches of vomited grief coming up from the bowels of my body – painful, visceral, devastating. And afterward, I felt nothing but wiped out.

As the months passed, then years, the quality and experience of the tears began to shift as well. After waves of emotion passed through my body, I would feel some sense of relief. Now, there is sweetness even during the tears. The moment of the tears marks the moment of the sweetness. Because every time I cry I'm accessing the deepest caverns of my heart space, and nothing – nothing – can be sweeter than that.

Now, I just want to cry my heart out. See that expression – how we language things? We know that certain pains live in the heart space – the pain of grief for example. We know that the heart is grief's abode. And when we experience grief in our lives and we're too afraid or too ashamed or possibly even too guilty to feel it... then our unwillingness to enter grief locks us out of our own heart space.

Which is where so many of us find ourselves. Locked out of that which we are. Adrift and searching out there for that which lies within. Until life slaps us down so strongly that we eventually begin to look within because there is nowhere else to go.

Awakening is nothing special. It's not even mystical, in so much as all of life is mystical. Awakening is simply knowing the truth of who one is. It is to see life as it is, nothing more, nothing less.

And yet we get caught, in our own elaborate dramas and plays and masks – all designed to protect us from feeling the pain of being human.

Why are we so afraid to feel emotional pain? Why are we so afraid to be emotional in front of other people?

Once upon a time, we didn't have verbal language. Sounds, possibly, but no words. When I feel back into that time... my sense is that survival depended on being able to sense the truth of another being, and it also depended on being able to hide the truth of our own being.

That within tribes where people loved and cared for each other, total openness would have meant that you just knew what other people were feeling, what they needed, and what they wanted. It was just known. It was safe to be open, and this led to connection and togetherness.

Yet if you were in a different kind of tribe, where it was all about survival and what you can get and beating your neighbour... being able to shut down and hide your emotional state of being would have also been strength. Shutting down would have been safe and powerful, and would have led to survival.

I feel into the Aboriginals of Australia, who traversed great distances over land they could read like words on a page, and I can sense the truth of their telepathic abilities. Imagine then, running into a people who were not broadcasting telepathically, and who used words with great disdain and dishonesty and only for their own ends.

How confusing. How heartbreaking.

* * *

It's impossible to compare my capacity to feel with another human being's capacity to feel, because how can I know how you sense life? I know I can sense all kinds of subtle information that appears invisible to most people, that I know things, just because. I know I cannot watch movies like *World War Z* because I experience the movie as if it were happening to me and being in the middle of a zombie invasion is not something I want to experience.

Was I always like this? Is this why, as a child, I shut down all ability to feel and sense the world around me and fled into my head, proudly choosing reason and rationality over messy emotion?

Am I any different than you?

Because, if the yogis are right and we are One, and the concept of separate beings is just an Illusion, then of course we can know everything that another knows. Of course we can communicate telepathically. Of course I can tune into my lover/not-lover in Europe and know what he is going through even though we're 12,000 miles away.

Of course.

Except this level of feeling is painful.

It's fucking painful.

So of course, because we are beings that are still mostly ruled by our lower chakras – beings that avoid pain and seek pleasure – of course we are going to shut down that entire plane of dimension, because being that tapped into everything and everyone... it fucking hurts.

Even as it is sweet. Even as it is blissful. Even as it changes, completely, the way you see life and relate to life and engage with life.

Waking up's a bitch, no doubt about it. Who the fuck would choose it? But there's no going back. Once you find out what the truth is, there's no Agent Smith who can make you forget. It just doesn't work that way.

The good news is, however, you can wake up AND still enjoy the steak.

We Are All the One

Whistler, 2004

Right before I woke up in 2004, I watched *The Matrix* series from beginning to end and took copious notes. I knew the first movie pointed at something profound – I could taste it. And I wanted to know if the series could take me all the way. Was it Truth?

But halfway through the last movie, with all that focus on Neo being the only one who can save everyone, I knew the filmmakers had lost their connection to Truth. That they'd been on to it, for a while, in a profound way... but then Maya had wrenched back control.

At least – that was my projection onto the movie series in that moment. Onto how Neo was being portrayed as the Saviour. My sense was that there is no such thing as a Saviour – as the One who is going to do something heroic or extraordinary that will save us all. That's bullshit, and feeds into a dynamic that sees people always looking outside of themselves for the One who is going to make everything better.

I knew – felt, sensed – that every single one of us is the One. We are all It. And we all have to do the work – however that looks in our lives.

There was one part in that last movie that I loved though. The moment when Neo baits Agent Smith into assimilating Neo, as he had assimilated the Oracle. And in doing so... that assimilation sent Neo's actual body back to The Source, which then ripples out into Agent Smith – he who has assimilated Neo – and white light bursts out of Agent Smith as he too is returned to The Source.

And Neo's last words are: "It was inevitable."

Just a movie. And I, watching that movie, am only going to see my own projections of what it means. Is that truth? Feel for yourself.

189

In my experience of reality, that final assimilation points to the integration of the Shadow side into the Light. That moment when a person finally stops projecting their own darkness out into the world and takes full responsibility for their own shadow. And of course, when the shadow is owned by the light, where does it go? What does it become?

Only those unable to handle their own pain will externalise that pain onto another. And the only people who do this are those who feel themselves as separate entities. Because when you know yourself as oneness, there is no 'out there'. Me, venting my pain on to you, still feels painful, because I feel your pain as if it were my own.

Those colonisers who left out food laced with poison for the Aboriginals to take and eat... were their hearts open? Did they know the truth of who they were? How could they? What kind of person can poison another human being? Surely only the kind of person who has a closed heart and who is cut off from the truth of who they are.

So many atrocities, around the world, in every moment.

And yet, when we pull back the lens even further, does it even matter if we die? When we die? How we die? If we are poisoned? Or gassed? Or beheaded? Or speared?

The yogis hold that fear of death is one of the kleshas – one of the obstacles to experiencing enlightenment. One of the obstacles to waking up.

There are five kleshas in total – ignorance, ego, aversion, attachment and fear of death. Ignorance is bliss – most people live in this space. Until they begin to wake up. And then they start to get a sense that who they are is not who they thought they were – their ego. The ego is the shell, the construct, the personality, the aspects of Self that are created as a way to survive in the world – as a way to avoid pain and seek pleasure.

We become people pleasers because we are terrified of an angry parent beating us. This is not who we are – it's a mode of operating in the world. And, at some point, it's a damn smart survival technique. There's nothing wrong with taking actions to avoid being beaten – especially as a child. The danger comes when it becomes an unconscious way of operating in the world, and a part of who we think we are.

A client said to me the other day; "I'm such a people pleaser."

I suggested she reframe that. "I have a pattern of people pleasing that I developed as a survival mechanism when I was a child."

Or simply, "I have a pattern of people pleasing."

Separating out our identity from our behaviour is the conscious removal of the second klesha – our misidentification with our ego. It's not about getting rid of our ego, or demonising our ego. Ego itself is a necessary way of interacting in the world – just like when Neo goes into the Matrix; he looks a particular way and wears particular clothing. But none of this is who he is. And once he wakes up, he doesn't mistake himself for the programme in the Matrix.

During psychosis I saw, very clearly, the programmes that were running in my system – and I knew they were not me. I felt the truth of who I was – the one watching it all. The one untouched by the Mind, going crazy. The One.

Ultimately, the same One that lives inside you.

That One is consciousness. During psychosis I felt it as Christ Consciousness. And even as I felt that, in the midst of the craziness, I saw how this knowingness of self as the One, as God, as Christ, could easily be hijacked by the ego. That is, if I still completely identified with the ego as myself. And I saw how this would show up as believing that I was special, that I was THE God, THE Christ. In other words: grandiose illusions.

My medical notes for Lion's Gate Hospital include a one-page printout that has a list of symptoms with a rating from 0 to 5. Grandiosity is one of those symptoms, because many people who experience psychosis have some kind of God delusion. It's common... oh so common.

My take on that? They're experiencing God consciousness, just as a yogi would during practice, but their identification with ego is still so strong that this experience becomes all about THEM.

In my case, I'd done enough practice to break that identification. So when I felt the energy of Christ Consciousness moving through my heart as if he was me and I was him, I witnessed it, I checked in, and I asked myself; 'What the fuck is going on here?' Right in the middle of my apparent psychosis.

Which points to exactly what Swami Shantimurti said – that the psych wards are full of people who've had some kind of awakening without the proper preparation for it, or without the context to work with and understand their experience.

Deep fucking gratitude for my yoga practice pre-2004.

Even though it likely also contributed to and triggered the awakening/psychosis before I was ready. That and the drugs. And my emotional patterns of suppressing what I was feeling, or speaking my truth. And sex.

Yeah, sex.

Can't really ignore that one anymore.

I suspect that my sexuality and sexual life was another reason why I woke up. Or went crazy.

And it tracks right back to when I was 16 years old and began masturbating. After I discovered my boyfriend – a much older boyfriend – had slept with his ex-girlfriend because I wasn't willing to have sex with him. The night I found that out, I went to bed and masturbated for the first time. My fuck you to his fucked up action, because he blamed my so-called prudishness for his sexual immorality.

It was the second time that had happened to me, even at such a young age.

My first boyfriend, also a good 7 or 8 years older than me, taunted me continually during our brief four-week relationship because I was reluctant to embark on sexual adventures with him beyond kissing. "Prude. Frigid." Yadda, yadda, yadda… All that crap men use to pressure women into having sex with them because they're unconsciously afraid that they are not attractive enough, and the unconscious pain of that causes them to attempt to coerce and control women to stop the pain of rejection.

I understood this dynamic then. I could feel it in him – in my boyfriend. Yet I wasn't feeling physically moved to engage with him past kissing, and I was holding to that.

But still, one night –barely 16 years old– I was in my boyfriend's bedroom and he was badgering me for sex – bad-ger-ing – so I finally said, "yes." This was after half an hour after saying, "no," but I wanted

192

to get the hell out of there and was scared he wouldn't take me home until I submitted.

Fucked up. Why didn't I just leave? Too good-mannered. Too afraid. Too socially conditioned into not creating a fuss. Too conditioned – by a well-meaning parent – to avoid owning and using my own anger as an appropriate boundary when necessary.

So I said yes. Even though I felt no. I lay back on the bed and endured, watching the clock on his bedside table tick-tick away, because I just wanted to get the hell home.

At least boyfriend #2 didn't pressure me. No, instead he just abandoned me to go and sleep with his ex-girlfriend. Proving that he didn't really give a shit about me and cared more about getting his rocks off. So yeah, I dumped his sorry arse immediately. And then set about getting to know myself sexually so I could prove once and for all that I wasn't frigid and I wasn't a prude.

What I didn't know at the time, as I systematically and thoroughly explored my sexuality and the way energy built and subsided and steadied and expanded and grew and finally tipped over into orgasm, was that I was using many yogic techniques to control my building orgasms. And I used those yogic techniques – particularly that of sahajoli – on a nightly basis, for years.

My approach to my sexuality was also like that of a yogi – scientific – using the body – my body – as the laboratory. I didn't so much lose myself in the experience as study it, with great concentration. That meant often focusing my awareness for long periods of time on certain points within the body.

Through these practices, muladhara is meant to wake up, and the kind of orgasm that a woman is able to have shifts from being in the nervous system – clitoral or vaginal – and instead becomes energetic – the spiritual or tantra orgasm.

My first conscious memory of experiencing this kind of energetic orgasm happened the first time I ever had sex with my fiancé. And it wasn't just one –he was the kind of guy that counts – it was something like 36.

Yes, 36 orgasms from one episode of sex. Not the kind of orgasms that wipe you out physically, but the kind that roll over and over and over each other and become one long drawn out wave of energetic orgasm where all sense of individual being-ness ceases to exist and all that remains is a giant ocean of sensation.

No wonder this man, intensely sexual himself, fell in love with me in a record two weeks.

And no wonder, as we embarked on the most sexually expressive relationship of my life, that my energetic system was blasted wide open into awakening/psychosis.

Where for art thou Home?

Laingholm, 2017

N ew Moon tonight.
I sat in ceremony, opening the directions, setting intentions,
playing *Voices of the Goddess*, a new album that showed up in my
inbox today. And then I practised.

As I sat in meditation, my hands came into the mudras of the
Bodhisattva and I began to weep... I want to go home. I want to go
home. I want to go home.

A yearning, for a place that is not here. That is not even a place.
Perhaps another lifetime, another dimension, another reality. I don't
know, not really. And yet I do, because the yearning is so strong, so
clear, so powerful.

I want to go home.

And I have been searching for that home.

Ever since I left home, age 18, off to Auckland for the University
summer break. Three months turned into 18 months and then I headed
overseas.

London, Chamonix, London, Niagara Falls, Whistler, Melbourne,
Whistler, Sydney, Whistler, Hawaii, Whistler and then back to New
Zealand.

And those are just the places I lived... not the places I travelled to,
or through.

Back in New Zealand, that craving for a home was compounded
by the sense of losing Whistler and separating from my Tribe. While I
always had a sense I couldn't make Whistler my real home, I also loved
that place and those people and felt bereft and adrift back in a land I

didn't want to return to. A land I had fled from, because I intuitively knew that fleeing from the land allowed me to flee from who I was meant to be, who I was expected to be.

Yet on my return to that land – to New Zealand – eight years to the day since my leaving, all that I left behind – the prison of those expectations – was waiting to claim me back. And so, resigned to being in that prison until I melted my way through the bars, one childhood pattern at a time, I searched physically for a place where I could feel at home, the way I'd felt at home in Whistler.

In three months, I traveled from Glenorchy to Auckland to Blenheim to Glenorchy and finally, to Queenstown. There, I found rest for almost three years until I moved in with Mr. Toastmasters in Arrowtown. It was not my first choice – Arrowtown felt oppressive and cramped by the hills that shaded the town through much of the winter, creating frost and ice that never melted. But Mr. Toastmasters lived there, in the house he'd built for his wife and daughter. But when he suggested we move to Wellington and seek our fame and fortune I was excited.

Maybe Wellington was the place where I'd finally feel at home.

* * *

Wellington, 2008

Four years after psychosis, and two years after starting teaching yoga, I finally found my sangha – my spiritual community. One Saturday evening, I went along to the Ashtanga Studio on Left Bank for a night of Kirtan – chanting. And I sat beside two women who I knew owned a local yoga studio. We got chatting. They were friends with the people leading the kirtan. That was the beginning of a circle of real and deep friendship that would sustain me through my relationship turmoil and single parenthood. Although it never felt like the Tribe I'd lost in Whistler, it did feel like I'd started to find a new kind of Tribe and a new way to feel connected to place.

But we didn't stay in Wellington long – it was down to Dunedin so my son's father could have shared care of his daughter. That only lasted nine months before we made plans to head back to Wellington. He missed the big city, and parenting half time was not what he'd thought it would be like. (All of which had made me realise that I couldn't parent my child with this man.) So a month before we left for Wellington, I left him – while on holiday in Glenorchy with my Mum. I stayed there, for a month, before heading back to Wellington solely because that was where my son's father had gone and I wanted them to be close.

Two months prior to our break-up, I'd had a dream that one of my friends from the Wellington sangha had beckoned me into her new house – asking me to live with her. I'd awoken with a start, as if the dream had happened. Yet I was living in Dunedin and still in a relationship.

Up in Wellington, I lived at another friend's beach house while getting my head around single parenthood. That friend was writing a book, and watching her at the kitchen table going through her editor's notes, I knew that a book wasn't far off for me too. I could feel it, taste it almost, gently flowing to me on the sea air.

Then that friend – the one from the dream – broke up with her husband and called me, suggested we move in together. So we did, with two other people. A house of the sangha, and a house that fed my soul. We held potlucks and kirtan and dance parties and yoga in the lounge, and nourished and fed each other food and love.

A year and a month after moving in, I went back down to Glenorchy for the school holidays to help my mother move house. She'd sold her house in anticipation of retiring at the end of the year and moving to Tauranga to live on my brother's property. In the meantime, she still had six months of the school year left as principal and was moving back into the school house – the same place she had been living when I first came back from Whistler in 2004.

This was July 2012 – eight years after. And as I helped my mother move, as the Glenorchy mountains watching over me, I felt a calling. I knew it was time to come back here. Not because I had no choice, like in 2004, but because now I did have a choice. And I had something else – a book ready to be born.

I returned to Wellington from that holiday knowing that change was coming. It was so palpable that I was afraid of something getting in the way – afraid of something stopping me from doing what I knew I had to do. Because I knew for sure now that it was a book calling me down to Glenorchy. By late September everything was in place and, yet again, my son and I loaded everything we owned into my Toyota Station wagon and headed south via my Dad's house in Blenheim and my sister's place in Christchurch.

Up the Islands, down the islands, up the islands, down the islands. How many miles have I traversed, looking for the home that is never there?

I arrived back in Glenorchy on October 5th 2012. Eight years to the day since arriving home from Canada. I even arrived back at the same house. And yet everything was different. I didn't immediately flee to the bathroom and collapse in a puddle of tears. I didn't turn my nose up in distain at the country bumpkins and their spring festival.

Instead, I marvelled at how everything was the same and yet I perceived it all differently. Held against the consistency of the town and the people, I could sense how much I had shifted and changed. Grown.

The book – my first book *Forty Days of Yoga* – wrote itself in four weeks, downloading verbatim as I walked around the Glenorchy Lagoon Loop track, the same track that I had pushed myself to run – orange marker by orange marker – in November 2004 as my only weapon against the post-psychosis depression that threatened to sink me forever.

Lack of childcare drove me from Glenorchy eighteen months later. Sam was about to turn four and the woman offering in-home early childhood care in Glenorchy stopped to have her next child. I tried driving to Queenstown – 40 minutes each way – and working at the library or a local cafe. But the commute wasn't sustainable and I could feel it was time to move.

Or maybe I was just searching for something. Maybe I was running from something.

Peter Sanson, the Ashtanga teacher, came through Queenstown. I took two classes with him. And decided to move to Napier and study with him.

Onward.

Napier didn't speak to my heart. I couldn't feel the land. I lasted six months, met one of my closest girlfriends, developed a new network of Napier friends, and then moved back to Wellington. Again. Third time lucky?

Onward.

It was nine months in Wellington before work obligations in the north made Tauranga attractive – that and the fact that my brother's family and mother lived there.

Onward.

Our first house was in Ohauiti. It sat only ten minutes from my brother's house, and a ten minutes bus ride for Sam to Oropi School. I still enjoyed Ashtanga yoga and found myself driving 35 minutes three times a week down to Mount Maunganui to go to classes there.

Onward.

Mount Maunganui, August 2015

Ah... finally...somewhere to stay. Sam was already attending his second school. He needed stability. Roots, we needed to put down roots. Yet it seemed that life kept unfolding in ways I had to surrender to... and by November 2016, Europe called. Six weeks to see if what Mr. Europe and I had was something real. Something worth pursuing. I could come up with the cash to fly Sam and I there... but I couldn't pay rent for six weeks while we were away. And I could feel Glenorchy calling again. Another book...

I gave up our house in the Mount, we went to Europe, and then came back to another station wagon packed with all our belongings and drove south, again.

Glenorchy, February 2017

Third time.

Back again.

My head spins, writing all this. Is that what this craving is... this deep longing... for that which I have never had in my adult life? For something mythical from childhood? For a feeling? For another world? For a home?

The book I thought I was going to write in Glenorchy stalled. Another book appeared – this one, but life was intense. While going through deep emotional processing of childhood beliefs and traumas I found it took all my focus and energy just to parent and keep my business ticking over.

And then there was Mr. Europe and I. He came for six weeks in April and May 2017. And a week after he went back to Europe, he spent the night with another woman. We know how that ended…

As you already know, my world, my future, my everything, blasted apart. I let him go. I let it all go. And I surrendered more deeply than I ever had before to whatever life might hold for me.

And now, I find myself here, in Laingholm, West Auckland, present day. Called up here by the land, by a friend's photos on Instagram.

Eight weeks on the ground, eight weeks of driving all over the city, and I feel like I might have finally come to a place I can stop. A place where I might be able to find that home I yearn for.

It's my third time living in Auckland. The first time, 19 years old, I was overwhelmed, and unconscious of the overwhelm. The second time, 29 years old, I was overwhelmed and conscious of it. Now, 42, I'm almost never overwhelmed. I'm rocking it.

Tonight, while sitting in meditation, tears poured down my cheeks, as I felt that yearning for a new life for Sam and I open up inside of me. I felt a new vision come forth. Of Sam and I creating a home together. Our own home. A family home, even though it's just the two of us.

Ever since I became a single parent, I've chosen to live with people – it's more financially viable and allows me some social interaction without having to leave the house. Smart huh?

Yet in the last week I've begun to suspect that unconsciously, I'm living with people because I'm trying to recreate the feeling of being a family. That I want to pull the people I live with into our family, because how can two people possibly make up a family? There's always a sense of someone – or someones – missing.

Tears. More tears. Oh truth how obvious you are with your ready emotion.

* * *

Whistler, 2000

The first time I ever had a glimpse of awakening was on magic mushrooms one night in Whistler, possibly around 2000.

Mushrooms were mega-fun, and my drug of choice in many ways. Non-toxic, non-chemical, and magical. The best drug of them all – and they grew naturally in the cow fields of Pemberton, thirty minutes north.

This time though, instead of the usual hilarity and reality-bending escapades, I was hit with the emotional impact of the loss of my family due to my parents' divorce. That was the beginning – the first crack in the dam of emotional resilience that had carried me forth through my teenage years and well into my twenties. It would only take another four years of drugs, sex and yoga before that dam imploded and sent me spiralling into psychosis.

That night, much to the bewilderment of my friends, a cohort of Aussie guys, my mushroom trip was soaked in tears as I felt that which I had lost, forever.

Family.

Belonging.

Connection.

Love.

Home.

Now you have it.

Now you don't.

How you going to cope with that, super-sensitive girl? That's right, just lock it all away in the depths of your heart and pretend that you don't care because you're tough, and rational, and have it all together. Pretend so well that you don't even know you're pretending.

That's going to work.

Until...

Until...

Until...

Sex, drugs and yoga.

Doesn't have quite the same roll of the tongue as sex, drugs and rock 'n' roll but it's oh so much more potent.

So yeah, back to the sex.

Worthless Piece of Shit

L et's talk about sex, baby. Starting with this.
You know what fucks me off?
Neo-Tantra. And how it's completely skewed the public's perception of what Tantra is all about.

If I were to claim any particular yogic lineage, it would be that of Tantra. Kashmir Shaivism possibly. Even though I've had scant interactions with teachers, and am far from being any kind of scholar. Yet when people ask what style of yoga I practice, I can't say 'Tantra' because then they think it's all about sex.

And that pisses me off.

As does taking one small aspect of the path of waking up and hijacking it for indulgent pleasure. Not that I really know if that's true – it's not like I've studied neo-tantra. I'm making it all up – all my shit. All my perception.

The thing with Tantra, in my limited understanding, is that all life as a whole is necessary component to waking up. Every little thing becomes grist for the mill, fuel for the fire, triggers for the understanding. It's never what you're doing, but how you're doing it and how awake you are while doing it.

There are two paths of Tantra – the right-handed and the left-handed. I know very little about either, except what I've gleaned from a few books. Left-handed is the path that embraces all there is and goes to town with mind-bending practices like creeping into cemeteries in the middle of the night to meditate while sitting on the body of corpses.

I get that.

What better way to contemplate the importance of life than while sitting on a corpse? Or while smeared in the ashes of a burned body? Because it's all just molecules. All just atoms. Any reaction we have is merely our own projection.

Just like my reaction to Neo-Tantra co-opting Tantra. Nothing more than a signal that I'm still attached somewhere in there, that I still have something to dissolve, let go of, realise.

Until that happens though, I'm content to own my fucked-off-ness. Tantra ain't sex.

Certainly, sex can be a fast-track ride to all kinds of bliss, which may or may not have something to do with yoga.

Whistler, 2002

Smack bang in the middle of my intensifying yoga and meditation practice, around 2002, I connected with the man who was to become my fiancé. We connected in a way that curled my toes all the way up into the crown of my head.

It wasn't even so much the mind-blowing sex – it was more subtle that that. It was the way we breathed together. Synchronicity with no effort – like one breath in two beings. In his arms, I found home. I also found multiple energetic orgasms that blasted open the realisation that something was going on in my spine. Something kinda weird. Something that felt a little like a snake. Or a lot.

I knew that, already, kinda. But until we started making love, this man and I, I'd regarded the spine tingling and 'popping' sensations of something rising up my spine to about L1 with curiosity more than anything else.

Then the sex started.

But what really blew everything up and away was the anal sex. Possibly even the DP – with a dildo. See, yogis work a lot with the perineum. Energetically, engaging the perineum is called mula bandha. A bandha is a lock – a way of moving energy up and around the body. One hallmark of Kundalini moving spontaneously around my body has been various locks showing up spontaneously, including Maha Bandha – the Great Lock. One minute, I'm just chilling out, possibly in meditation, next minute, my body is moving into a Bandha and holding it for a fucking long time.

All I can do is surrender to the movement, surrender to the energy, just fucking surrender.

Turns out that anal sex is also some kind of bandha. Of course, anal sex kicks off the yogic flow with a bang, because it requires total surrender – to resist is fucking painful. Take that full surrender of the body whilst also practicing sahajoli and focusing all of one's attention on the bindu located in muladhara... and fuck me... While all I can offer is experiential insight... I swear, anal sex felt like a giant reset button.

Like with every thrust my entire operating system was being turned off and on in a way that completely reset my nervous system.

Plus, what made this experience of anal sex so damn potent was that I was completely in love, devotion, service and surrender to this man. I adored him, and had opened up to him on every level – except daring to tell him the truth about a couple of key factors, like that I didn't really want to have threesomes with other women.

I sublimated myself to him.

Total surrender.

Which was diametrically in opposition to how I had always been – rigidly in control.

From a psychological perspective, this was a 180-degree shift in my operating system. A complete overhaul. And my theory is that our voracious and varied sex life completely reset my nervous system, and was one of the contributing factors to the breakdown of my psyche. My emotional holding patterns were interrupted because all that surrender on the deepest possible psychosomatic level meant that I could no longer hold back the dam on my suppressed reality.

Because in addition to completely sublimating and surrendering to this man, I was also denying my own truth and giving away my power.

Add in acid, mushrooms, ecstasy and pot and voila! Psychological breakdown everywhere! Oh, and Kundalini of course, with all her spontaneous kriyas and weird languages, visions and prophetic insight.

What. A. Ride.

* * *

Now... sex is generally either very connected and heart open, or kinda mechanical and hum drum. I'd love to say that with my awakening self that I've consistently made conscious sexual decisions in the last decade. But I haven't. Sex and relationships have continued to be my precipice – the edge where I'm most unconscious, and where I fall down the most.

Wellington, 2014

Despite apparently being able to sense so much about the nature of reality, I've done dumb shit: I once went out on a date with a man I found interesting and yet not particularly attractive. And when he kissed me and I wasn't really into it... I thought to myself, 'I'm obviously not drunk enough'... so proceeded to get drunk enough to handle kissing him some more... before allowing him to put us in taxi to my place where we had shitty drunken sex.

Why? Because he intrigued me as a friend and I didn't want to lose our friendship.

What. The. Fuck?

About three days before this happened, I had a dream about this man and I hanging out, and in that dream, I had this weird protuberance on my lower belly like some kind of belly fat roll that looked like the edge of a flying saucer.

Right after that man left my bed and caught a taxi home, mercifully as soon as we'd finished having sex, I felt an intense wave of sensation in the low belly radiating out exactly like the protuberance in the dream.

Only now, in real life, I could feel what that emotion was.

Shame.

I

Felt

Ashamed.

And as I felt the shame of my behaviour and actions wash over me... I realised that likely, I had felt this shame many, many times in my life before but I had been too unconscious and too shut down to know.

So that's what shame felt like! First time ever, feeling shame – 2014, 38 years old. That's how repressed I've been in my life.

And it took that shitty situation with this guy where I made shitty choices before I could finally feel the shame that had always been there. I guess it had to play out, because one thing I've realised about this damn

206

Kundalini ride, is that it's all about making the unconscious conscious. If I'm not able to do it in my practice and on the mat, sometimes I'll find myself in shitty situations like that wondering what the fuck I'm still doing acting like a dumb-arse, drunken 20-year-old.

Why did I act like that? Why did I deliberately get drunk so I could handle kissing a guy I didn't really feel attracted to? Because I felt worthless. Because I felt that the only 'value' I had was sexual. That's why. And I knew it, afterwards.

Worthless. At my core. In my heart. A deep wound, carried from childhood. A wound that I lived out, healed and released in graphic detail in May of 2017.

Although, the deep dive into the wound began earlier than May. It began in February, when I returned to Glenorchy to write and found myself plummeting into the darkness almost immediately. What the fuck? Was I doomed to always feel like shit? What was going on? I caught it, fast. Through witnessing myself (of course), I noticed that I also appeared to be super motivated to churn out work – make videos, write articles, post on social media. I watched this dual thing going on – feeling like absolute shit while also being all inspired and motivated – and I wondered...

Is this connected?

And then I noticed the parallels between the last two times I had lived in Glenorchy – in 2004 and 2012. Both times, I had frantically thrown myself into work projects. In 2004, I felt like a failure, and was desperately trying to prove I wasn't. In 2012, I'd come down to write a book, and I was parenting a 2-year-old all by myself because Mum had retired and moved to Tauranga. My son would go to childcare at 10am and I would walk around the boardwalk, clearing my head and downloading the day's work. Once home, I'd sit at my laptop and work straight through until 4pm, usually skipping lunch because I didn't want to waste a precious moment. Then I'd pick him up, play badly (because I suck at kid's play) make dinner, do the bedtime routine and get him to bed by 7pm. Then I'd jump back on my laptop and work until 10pm before crashing, exhaustedly into bed myself.

That's how I managed to write, edit, and self-publish a book in something like five months.

In February 2017, there I was, back in Glenorchy, writing a book again, and feeling like a piece of shit.

Noticing that.

Sitting with that.

Working with that.

Oh, and the book wasn't happening, not in the way it was meant to. No four-week super-easy download this time around.

Then Mr. Europe came over for five weeks, as we were teaching a retreat in Taupo in May. We'd been together for almost a year by then, and the plan was that he'd comes to NZ for five weeks, and Sam and I would head over to Croatia in September for three or so months. We were edging towards somehow creating a round-the-world life together.

Mr. Europe and I went camping.

At Lake Middleton.

A place of mythical proportion in my personal history.

This is where we camped as a family from as long as I have memories. Right through the divorce, when Mum stopped coming and my step-Mum started coming, along with her two kids. All the way until I was about 17 years old. That's ten or fifteen years of memories, as a child and teenager, tied to one place.

Plus, there was that one time I went there with my first love and we had sex for the first time ever. Well, it wasn't my first time; because there had been that utterly unenjoyable time two years prior. But I didn't count that, because you've got to want to, right? For it to count?

Lake Middleton, 2017

So there Mr. Europe and I are, in late April – autumn here in NZ – camping with Sam. He's sleeping in my kitted-out van, and Mr. Europe and I have put up this awesome two-room tent that Dad and my step-mum gave me for my birthday one year.

It's surreal, being there, feeling the land and the trees and the lakes. A place I knew as only children can know a place – and yet it's almost 40 years later. But it feels like a home to me. Eerie. Poignant.

Night falls early, and being camping, there's nothing to do once Sam's in bed but to go to bed. We're reading a book – together, out loud. And so Mr. Europe and I nestle into bed with cellphones as a light source and take turns reading from Jed McKenna's *Enlightenment Trilogy*. I think we're on book #2 – the one where he gets all obsessed about *Moby Dick*.

We're also taking the odd sip of a bottle of Jack Daniels. Now, something I've been observing with interest since I got to Glenorchy in February is that I'm drinking. Almost every night. Maybe one or two glasses of red wine. Or a whiskey. Or something. I'm watching myself do this, and I know that something is up.

That's Tantra, right there. Notice how I don't judge myself for drinking. I don't think about whether I should or shouldn't be drinking, or whether I'm bad. I don't feel guilty. I just notice what's up. That something inside of me is making me reach for the bottle.

So, camping… A couple slugs of whiskey go down during the reading and then it's lights out. We fall asleep around 11pm.

11:35pm I wake up.

Wide awake.

Sit up.

Mr. Europe's awake instantly too – he wakes up if a leaf falls off a tree.

"What's up?"

Tears are rolling down my face and I hunch over and hold myself. "I'm… I'm… a child again eight or so years old… I can feel myself… in my tent. I'm a child and I…"

Mr. Europe's sitting up now too. "What?"

"I feel like an absolute worthless piece of shit."

And I do, it's rolling through my body as a visceral body memory of something I couldn't feel then that's breaking through the time barrier and making itself known to me right now. I'm also feeling very, very, very sick.

"Hang on, I'm getting a bucket!" Mr. Europe's up and out the tent door.

"I'm not going to throw up!"

He's back, bucket in hand thrusting it under my face. Tears and snot run down my chin as I shiver and wail over and over again. "I feel like an absolute worthless piece of shit."

And I begin to vomit. Like I'm sixteen and drank too much whiskey. Only I know that I only had a few sips. Okay, maybe gulps. They were gulps, because I could feel the energy behind how I drank – a desperate need to suppress something and keep it down out of my awareness. But it's all coming back up now. "I feel like an absolute worthless piece of shit."

Over and over and over again I spew the words out as I empty my guts with tears and snot streaming down my face and into the bucket. Mr. Europe holds energetic space, and my hair, allowing me to purge out something I've carried inside myself for over three decades.

This goes on, and on, and on, and on. For a couple of hours maybe. "I feel like an absolute worthless piece of shit."

And then finally, it's done. No more vomit. No more tears. Still plenty of snot coming through. But by now we've found the tissues and I've managed to clean up my face.

The vomit bucket goes outside and I fall into an exhausted sleep. Healing process complete, some 30 or so years later. Because once upon a time, as a young girl, lying asleep in a tent at Middleton, I felt like an absolute worthless piece of shit. But those feelings would have been too painful to feel, so I suppressed them, afraid they were true. Shoved them away, locked deep down inside of me.

There's no recall of why I felt like that. Not then, in May 2017. It's not until a year later, when I share that story at a weekend workshop in Wellington, that the memory attached to the emotion floats into my awareness.

And that's what's most fascinating. We don't need to know the why to heal the trauma and release the limiting belief. We don't need to know the story, we don't need to figure it out or understand anything. We just need to let the body do its work.

The body always knows. And the body doesn't care about timeframes. Returning to the scene of the crime brought me back into an emotional reality that I'd unknowingly suppressed. And, it was an emotional reality that, for much of my life had likely driven so many of my apparent 'free' choices and decisions. Not until we know ourselves can we live consciously. Until then, we are mere programmed machines. Robots. Stuck in the Matrix, living out lives we believe are our own, but which are really the product of all we believe ourselves to be.

Worthless. I'd always believed – and feared – that I was worthless.

That belief was installed into my system the first summer we stayed at Lake Middleton. And possibly that feeling of worthlessness was ingrained into me by countless small actions over a number of years. That's how beliefs work – our lives seek to reinforce what we believe, because the beliefs feel safe and true.

It's gone now, though, that belief of being worthless.

I puked it out.

And with it, I got rid of all kinds of behaviour patterns, fears and insecurities. Including sleeping with men I wasn't attracted to because I thought it was a good thing to do. 'Cos you know… worthless.

The Mystic and the Scientist

And in the end, that's all this awakening business seems to have been about.

Seeing who I am, and what I am not.

Why it all happened, to me, is almost irrelevant. The awakening experiences were merely mystical experiences. And they're as common as chicken shit on a chicken farm. Something like 60% of all Americans report having had one – no big deal. Okay, not everyone ends up in a psych ward. That was just my own particular, branded version.

After it all went down, and my perspective of life was irrevocably shifted, I thought that this was just the evolution of humanity – the awakening part, not the psychosis part. That eventually we'd all have these experiences and wake the fuck up.

Now, I'm not so sure.

Now, I've come to realise that perhaps there is something about me that is different.

Not special, mind you. Just different. In the way that an actor is different from a brain surgeon.

One word that fits is mystic. But being a mystic also means I don't easily fit into today's world. I see and feel things that ordinary folk don't. I used to believe that eventually everyone would see and feel the same things I did, believing that made me feel safe and comfortable for a long time. Even when weird shit kept happening to me, like that time my boyfriend and I were making love and a Lion God came down and used his body, or became his body, or something…

Like many of these experiences, it's difficult to articulate exactly what happened. Except that it involved making love, with a real physical man, whose body was suddenly also inhabited by that of a Lion God. And I was stone cold sober. I hadn't touched intoxicants for years.

213

So, those kinds of experiences roll through me, not infrequently. With them, I get knowingness of things to come. A way of sensing the world that is inexplicably subtle. None of it's special – I know, I've already said that but's it's fucking important to me. Just as some people have a talent for dance, I have a talent for the subtle.

That's the mystic in me. Or possibly the medicine woman. Because another name for the experience I went through in 2004 is Shaman's Sickness – that experience that in tribal society marks out the ones who are to become their tribe's shamans, tohunga, medicine men and medicine women. The ones who could read the subtle. The ones who can see beyond, feel beyond, and hold space for everyone else in the tribe. The ones who can heal, on the level of consciousness.

Often those who became shamans had some kind of mysterious illness as a child or young person that marked their entry into the world of the subtle. Of course, when that happened, the elders would know what was happening and support the emerging shaman by any means necessary.

Nowadays, those emerging shamans are likely to get labelled mentally ill, medicated and/or locked up in a psych ward.

* * *

I had a session with a client last week. A young woman who's had a break from reality. Psychosis. Visions. She's confused, ungrounded. And on anti-psychotics. Working with her, I had a clear sense of her as a Seer. I had a sense of the apprenticeship that she is ready for. A sense of how she needs to be guided and strengthened. A sense of the context she requires to make sense of her experience. All of this was clear to me.

That's my mystic, my medicine woman, knowing things, seeing things.

That's the one who read *the Bible* from cover to cover when she was 8 years old because... because why? Who reads *the Bible* from cover to cover? Especially as a child! Me, that's who. I picked up that very same Bible – I got it for Christmas the year I was eight and it still sits on my bookshelf – and I flicked through. Holy fuck! I don't know if I could read through it now. But I did it as an eight year old – every single book, except Psalms. And that's how I know, for sure, that I did read it all – because I remember so clearly getting to the Psalms and pausing. Songs, in written form. Bloody boring. And yet I wanted to read it all – perhaps needed to read it all – so I debated with myself. And then skipped Psalms because reading a bunch of old songs totally sucks ass when you're eight years old. So I skipped Psalms but I kept reading, all the way through to the end of Revelations.

Yet there is also the scientist in me. The one who observes and questions and comes up with theories. The one that is never too attached to anything and is willing to be proven wrong. Because after I read *the Bible* and observed the Church and everything that went down inside that institution... I decided that it was all a load of bollocks. What I read... and what the Church was... didn't stack up. So in my early teens, I became an atheist, a sceptic and a rationalist.

Then came yoga. Twenty-one years old and after my first class... I just knew. I'd found something. Whatever it was that I'd been searching for in *the Bible*, I knew, this was where I'd find it.

Of course, yogis are the ultimate scientists *and* the ultimate mystics. They use the laboratory of their own body to know themselves as God. Or to know God as themselves. Because when it all comes down to it, in that moment of oneness, in that experience, there is no Seeker, no Knower, no... anything left. You become God but YOU'RE not there either.

Nowadays, mystical experiences beckon me from inside every moment – all I need do is stop thinking. Which appears to be coming easier and easier. It's just a shift of focus away from the tool of the Mind and instead into Self as consciousness. And then a sense of expanding the sense of Self outward into all that surrounds me. Thoughts only hold me hostage when there's an emotional trigger still caught somewhere in there. They've become a signal of some fear ready to be seen, embraced, released, and let go...

Fear is still a worthy foe however. I can still find myself subsumed in fear... yet I am also able to witness it, and ask myself the all-important question:

'What am I believing that is not true?'

Because when I'm aligned with Grace and God and in knowingness, Fear ceases to exist.

In truth, it's all a Jedi Mind trick.

Where am I?

Who am I?

What am I?

Ah fear... lead me home... lead me home to that which I truly am.

Maybe this is the home I was yearning for the other night. The home where I know the truth of who I am... where I am one with God. For what other home could ever exist? Anything in the material world is only a pale facsimile of this place. That home feels like the place I've yearned for, ever since I was born. Suggesting that my 'forgetting' at birth was not as complete as it could have been. That when I was born, I remembered what it was like to not be born.

Perhaps this is the way it is meant to be. That when consciousness erupts again into human form – into physical form – there is a sense, a remembering, a knowing of being One with All that remains. It remains as the seed, the scent, or the desire designed to lead us back into that place of home that lies within human form.

A giant, cosmic joke as it were. So many of us seek to find that place of home – connection, belonging, love, and acceptance – out there... when really, it can only ever be found in here. And then, once we find it in here, how can we not manifest and magnify it out there, over and over and over again?

How could I not be at home anywhere in the world, once I am at home with my Self and God, Consciousness, the Divine (choose your favourite word)? Where could I possibly be outside of this place of Home? How could I ever possibly be lost again?

Ah but... that's the thing, isn't it? Because likely I will become lost again, and again, and again. Every time I lose that faith and trust in who I am... I lose God. I lose home. I lose...

But every time I come back, I remember how to come back, and the remembering of coming back becomes stronger and stronger and stronger and I am gone for shorter and shorter and shorter times until...

Abiding self-realisation.

Perhaps not just for the spiritual greats amongst us.

Perhaps for all of us.

Actors and brain surgeons and mystics and scientists alike.

Yes, I just contradicted myself… because perhaps I am wrong and we are all mystics and this is the natural evolution of humanity.

Because who doesn't want to know themselves as God and know God as themselves?

Who doesn't want to feel abiding peace even as difficult and uncomfortable emotions surge through the body?

Who doesn't want to feel safe and at home, no matter what their life circumstances?

Who doesn't want to know themselves as Love?

I do

because

I AM.

And that is all.

* * *

Only it's not all.

There's more.

There's the hundreds and thousands of other people having awakening experiences conflated with psychological disturbances, people who don't have the context that I had for my experience. People who get caught up in the Western Medical model and end up on anti-psychotics as the sole treatment for their experience, with possibly a little talk therapy if they're lucky, and shock therapy if they're not. People who experience the multi-dimensional nature of life and can't ground and contain the experiences, so they blow out their wiring and end up in the psych ward. Trapped.

And without the context and understanding that I had, they also have additional layers of anxiety, depression and fear about who they are and who they are not. Confused with all the projections and ideas of mainstream society about mental illness and spiritual emergence.

People like the gentleman who happened into my yoga class once upon a time. He was wearing an old loose, mustard-coloured, possibly-home knit jumper and a pair of old man trousers – the kind my Pop used to wear. But this man wasn't that old. He might not even have been fifty, despite shuffling along with his shoulders hunched over. I recognised that shuffle and it wasn't the shuffle and hunch of old age. It was the shuffle and hunch of medication, and of a man trying to hide away from seeing how other people see him.

He had a diagnosis, this man. Was given it in his early twenties when he had some kind of breakdown. But I didn't see that diagnosis. I saw the man, and the boy, and I felt his heart. It was big, and unbounded, even within the tightness of his body and the cage of the medication.

He came to a handful of classes, peering up at me from underneath his hair as he manoeuvred his body this way and that amongst the lycra-clad women who dominated my classes. He watched intently, listened to every word and every nuance. Saw everything.

Never was I more aware of my languaging than when I taught with this gentleman in my class. I spoke for him and to him even though everything I said was addressed generally to the class. It was an honour and a gift to have him in my class and I wanted to do him justice, because this could be the only yoga class he ever experienced. I wanted him to know that the way he showed up was perfect, just as he was – inflexible, stiff, uncoordinated, groggy and all. And I saw, over that tiny number of classes, the impact the teaching had on him. What it meant to him to be seen as a man, and accepted, and loved, just as he was.

I saw him light up, I saw words land just so in his heart, I saw his pleasure at being seen and accepted.

In my class, this man wasn't mentally ill. He was a human being finding his way back home in a system that was failing him. That had failed him.

Because when the system sees mental illness as something to be treated as an aberration, medicated and shutdown, rejected, locked away and vilified… we condemn hundreds and thousands of human beings to a life – and often a death – of unnecessary suffering.

We stop people from using their experiences as a way into greater wholeness, and as a way into their gifts.

This man stopped coming after four or five classes. Family reasons. After nearly three decades in the system with his classification... I knew it was unlikely he'd ever find the road to healing and recovery that I found. It was too late for him.

But it might not be too late for you. Or your brother. Or your daughter. Or your neighbour. Or your work colleague.

There is a way through mental illness that leads to wholeness, and I'm not the only one who has found it.

That way has meant turning toward my brokenness as the gateway to wholeness.

It has meant training myself to feel my emotions when they happen, rather than locking them away deep inside, or ignoring them, or running away from them, or distracting myself.

It has meant noticing when I'm resisting life, and when I'm resisting how I'm feeling, and instead choosing to feel the truth of my experience and choosing to be in life as it's unfolding.

Even the hard, painful stuff.

Especially the hard, painful stuff.

It's the pain that leads to freedom.

That's the secret.

That is...

...the secret.

Multi-Dimensional Reality

Laingholm, 2017

The road to wholeness can take some unexpected turns though – turns that have even freaked me out. Like that energy/entity that I've been sensing for over a decade now. What the fuck is that? It's definitely not something I would ever go and see my doctor about.

"So yeah, there's this thing inside me, on my right side, that feels like some kind of dark, evil Elvis. Complete with lip-curl. I'd like him extracted please. Or exorcised. Or you know, whatever."

With my history, it would be back to the psych ward, quick smart. So yeah, nah.

Not going to open that conversation with anyone in the medical profession anytime soon. But it is a conversation I have with my healer friends, and my tohunga friend, and my fellow shaman/seers/sages.

In the shamanic worldview, including that of Māori, entities are very real, and shamans and tohunga have specific processes for dealing with them. My scientist wonders… are entities a physical manifestation of sensations arising from negative thought patterns, triggered by stored emotion? Are they thought forms that take on emotional and physical attributes? Is this the same thing, described in different words?

Because that's the thing with spiritual emergence and mental health. When we learn to listen to people's experiences as if they are true and real – which they are, for them – then, through that deep listening and acceptance, we can start to feel into the truth of what is happening through a different lens – say a psychological lens. Because the psychological lens and the mystical lens and the shaman's lens are often all seeing the same thing, but language-ing it in different ways.

221

And through listening deeply to the weird and wonderful experiences that people are having... we can find the pathway to wholeness. So often it lies through the content of our experiences – content that the Western Medical model usually dismisses. Delusion. Hallucination. Voices.

Well yeah, AND that shit is real. It points to things. It points to the healing the psyche needs. Follow it! Learn how to track it! Learn how to decipher it! Trust it! Know it!

But doing this work – the tracking and the deciphering and the trusting and knowing – is all the more challenging because without an ability to ground and contain, accessing shaman's reality can tear the uninitiated away from all reality.

Even as recent as 2017, when I would allow myself to drop into trance states –shaman's reality, when Kundalini would lead – I was still afraid I was crazy. And I would video myself, so I could show the videos to a couple of close friends and make sure that I wasn't.

"Nah, you're not crazy. Fuck – you're one of the sanest people I know!"

In those states, my psyche was unwinding itself. Unfolding. Unfurling. Just as it was back in 2004.

And that's what inspired me to finally bring this work to the world. Because I am sane, fucking sane, even as I experience a multi-dimensional reality that many medical professionals would say is at best a highly active imagination and at worst delusional.

The strong emotional processes, the weird sounds and strange body movements are simply the evolution of consciousness at play.

I know that now.

And so I've written this story so that other men and women like myself can benefit from my story. So other people can benefit from the context that I used to heal and recover. Because yeah, it took a fucking long time for me to make it through. But I made it. I made it all the way out the other side and into fucking awesomeness. I made it so far through that I can CHOOSE to step into multi-dimensional reality at any time, while staying grounded and contained. And, I can choose to walk in ordinary reality unseen.

There are so many of us in this world now – so many shamans and healers and sages and shining lights.

There are so many, because this planet is shifting. Consciousness is shifting. We are the pioneers, the ones on the fringes, pushing the edges and exploring new territory.

We are the ones with awakened Kundalini going through all kinds of weird and strange experiences that we're petrified mean that we're crazy.

But we're not.

We're not crazy.

You just need to see us through different eyes.

You need to see us through the eyes of consciousness, not through the eyes of the material.

We are called, as Awakened Heart Warriors, to walk in both worlds, to bridge the worlds, to be lantern-bearers, to light the way.

We are called to light each other's way. We are called to inspire each other and support each other. To become more than we are, so that we may serve others like us who are going through spiritual emergence and who need context and containment and grounding.

Because there are many, and there will be many more.

This is the Awakening.

* * *

Last night, I did a ceremony for a friend who also walked this path. It began with cleaning my room and clearing the space. I packed my jasper pipe – bought in Mexico this July for the purpose of ceremony – using homegrown, natural marijuana. The Grandmother. Candle lit, altar prepared, eyes closed, intention set. I sat on my bed, window wide open, listening to the sounds of the forest, bowing my head, before lighting the bowl. Three inhales, holding kumbukha with each one and feeling the Grandmother enter my consciousness, before finally exhaling slowly.

Then I sat, before my altar, and began my practice. When I ask the Grandmother to guide me, this is the crucial aspect. Setting up the strongest possible container so I can travel safely beyond the worlds.

Without this container, it is too easy to get lost, to wander further than one can hold. That's where visioning ends and psychosis begins. Because the nature of the plant guide means that it exacerbates whatever is already going on in the psyche.

Yes, it increases my ability to perceive, and to vision, and to know. But it also fuels the thoughts and draws up anxieties and fears, and paranoia. When I'm able to stay connected to All that Is, I can skilfully work with all these things – the obsessive thoughts, the anxieties, the fears and the paranoia. But if I begin to shift out of All that Is, and into my mind, I'm lost.

The distinction is crucial.

And it's why people who are natural Shamans, Healers, Sages and Seers need to be very cautious and mindful when using plant medicine guides like Marijuana. It's a discipline, like anything else.

My practice began, and the rhythm of my breath and the movement of my spine anchored me into presence even as The Grandmother began to take me on journeys. I know that I've gone too far when I suddenly realise I've dropped out of the breath work and movement of my practice. The moment I notice, I connect again to my breath and move once more.

Breathing, moving, chanting, and feeling into the essence of my friend, so we may connect on the astral plane. Or the causal realms. Or something. Last night, it was my friend's heart I felt the most – his particular quality of masculinity. It's an aspect of being that hasn't come naturally to me in the past, yet thanks the close and intimate friendship we have, I now have access to it.

The first time I noticed this friend entering into my being was last September, as I led a Great Emptying Out Women's Retreat. We were sitting in circle, while I worked with one woman in particular. As she shared, and I guided her deep into the truth of her being, I felt my friend with me. I felt his presence within me. I felt his heart and his love and his care and it blossomed within my heart and came through me. After, I gave a prayer of thanks for his support.

Last night during the ceremony… it was the same thing. I felt his presence enter into my field. There he was, with me, becoming me. And as I felt him, I had a sense of unity consciousness. Of how when we open to each other on the deepest level, on the most subtle level, as I did in this ceremony, that we can feel each other as if we ARE each other.

Because we are each other.

Those of us who are awakening feel, deeply, the hearts of all beings.

Or, as another of my friends messaged to me yesterday, "We feel too much."

To that I say NO! We don't feel too much! It's simply that in this lifetime we haven't been trained or initiated into the abilities required to hold and process and use that feeling sense.

Now, I have been trained and initiated through my yoga practice and my healing journey, I am capable of feeling the strongest of emotions and still staying anchored in the Witness.

Now, I know and understand that I inhabit a multi-dimensional world that is consciousness based. It is not the mechanistic, Newtonian world of my culture. It is the world of the indigenous peoples. That is my world. I am a Medicine Woman. Shaman. A Healer. A Sage. I feel and know truth. I serve something beyond me, which moves through me with purpose.

This is my life. And I claim it. I claim it for all the people living in the multi-dimensional world, and for those who don't yet know it. All those who are lost and those who are finding their way back.

I claim it for us all.

So we may live here together, knowing who we are, and sharing out gifts in a world that understands us.

Sun Shine

My alarm went off this morning and I was not ready, I was tired. That made me grumpy. Yet the grumpiness was a thin veneer stretched over a pulsing heart of joy and aliveness.

The kind of joy and aliveness that didn't exist in me when I began writing this book, in September 2017. The act of putting these words down, of chasing these lines through my memories and fears helped me cross a barrier that had been eluding me for 13 years.

What happened?

I don't know, exactly. Although I do remember the moment when I noticed that something had changed. I was in Tauranga, staying with my Mum and brother. My Mum and I were out for lunch, with Sam. We ate smoked salmon, at a long wooden table, watching an even longer line of traffic through the wide windows. The traffic wended around a roundabout and the conversation meandered this way and that, mostly centred on my realisation that it was time for Sam and I to find our own home.

"He's eight now... and I want to create a home for him before it's too late – our own place, with a dress-up box and a circus props box. And a kitten, and dance parties, and dinner parties..."

As I shared our plans with my mother, joy bubbled up in my heart. This was happening. We were finally going to get our own home. And this time, I knew, we had found the place to live. Laingholm was it, for at least a few years.

Was this why I felt the joy? The optimism? The happiness? Because, yes, it was happiness, surging sweetly through my system.

Thing is, the home hadn't happened yet. It was just an idea, a concept, that I started sharing with my Mum over lunch that December day. And three months on, it still hadn't happened. We'd been applying for houses, and getting turned down, but even that hadn't blocked the flow of joy and optimism and happiness though.

So it's not the external circumstances, because of course, it's never the external circumstances that create joy. It's only ever what's inside of us... and I've found something inside of me. I've dropped back into my power. Into my truth.

And it might have something to do with what happened when Mr. Europe, my lover/ex-lover/again-lover/ex-lover, came to New Zealand in November. I'd already realised, three weeks prior, that he wasn't the man for me. I'd held him through his grief as he felt like I rejected him. And now he was coming to NZ because we had four events booked – a mini-tour – and I saw it as an opportunity to develop a new foundation of friendship to move from.

Only it didn't happen like that.

It got messy.

Real messy.

There were arguments and yelling and confusion and I got sick in the middle of it all – bedridden sick – and he was staying in my house and my room and my bed still. I was beginning to see and understand the co-dependence and unconscious power dynamics that had defined – and fuelled – our relationship. Subtle. Hidden. Yet strong as fuck. And through it all, I could see that as long as I behaved in a particular way, everything was okay. The moment I was upfront and honest about my needs and desires, it wasn't okay.

* * *

The breakthrough came on Thursday night. My friend Nik was over for dinner. And Mr. Europe and I dialogued as we always did, even though Nik was there. We named what was going on, as much as we could. And there was a fuck load going on. It felt to me that Mr. Europe just wasn't listening to me at all. It felt like he was stuck... stuck being angry with me, stuck bullying me, stuck controlling me.

As we talked it all out, Nik listened, and mediated, and offered a much-needed third perspective.

In the midst of it all – in the midst of Mr. Europe yelling and me explaining... I said, "You just have to let me GO." And I burst into tears, out of nowhere, blurting out as I FELT it in the cells of my body. "You don't know what it's like to be owned by a man."

And there it was. On some deep cellular level, even though I'd broken up with Mr. Europe – twice now – I still felt like he OWNED me. Like he could do anything he wanted to me, and with me, including kill me.

It wasn't rational.

And it was real as fuck.

I had touched into some deep feminine ancestral or collective memory of what it feels like to be owned by a man. And on an unconscious level, my dynamic with Mr. Europe was defined by a sense of being owned BY him.

Because until this century, in much of the world, women WERE owned by men. We were handed from father to husband, bartered and sold, claimed and raped. Hell, it STILL happens. That night, attempting to untangle myself from Mr. Europe, that's what I felt in my cells – like he owned me.

I felt it. I named it. And then it was gone.

The next day, I asked for space. A friend's house was empty, just down the road. Please go and stay there for a few days.

Mr. Europe responded by changing his flights and fleeing the country within 24 hours. Leaving me to deliver the rest of our events, including a three-day retreat, by myself. My business – those events – had paid for his flights. But he didn't care. Couldn't care. He was in a world of hurt of his own that had nothing to do with me, and he wasn't capable of showing up to his responsibilities in any way.

I was left holding it all.

I went into shock – that someone I had worked with and loved and lived with so closely over the last eighteen months could abandon his responsibilities in such a way. But even in the middle of the emotional intensity, and the financial fallout, and the impact on my business... I knew this was a final test. An initiation. And so I felt and fought my way through, aligning to my values.

I emailed the eleven people who had signed up and paid for the retreat and offered everyone a full refund, while telling them about the new retreat I was going to offer in the same space and time. Six people chose to come anyway, and I led my first healing retreat by myself.

And while I dealt with the real-world fallout, internally I reviewed every single interaction between Mr. Europe and I – particularly the disagreements we'd had while working together. And I began to see the pattern. I would raise something that didn't feel right to me, and he would brush it off, or explain it away, or justify it... and instead of me staying clear about what I knew – what I could FEEL was true – I allowed myself to be persuaded to ignore my knowingness.

I chose to trust him, over me. I bowed to his view, his ideas, his perspective, his way.

Power. It was all about power.

I had unconsciously given my power away to Mr. Europe, consistently, throughout our relationship. Just as I had given it away to every man I had ever been with. That deep cellular sense of being owned by a man... it had lived in me my whole life and I had acted as if it were true. As if the men I chose to be with owned me, and by extension, owned my gifts and talents and power. I'd handed it all over to them, while buying into and believing their perspective of reality.

Seeing that, naming that, owning that...

That was when my joy started coming back.

That was when I started feeling alive again.

That was when I started to feel happy again.

* * *

After the psychosis, after my fiancé dumped me, after coming back to New Zealand... I'd vowed that I'd never sacrifice myself for a man ever again. That I wouldn't give up who I was to make a man happy.

It's taken thirteen years or more to bring that vow to fruition. Because I did sacrifice myself to my son's father – I gave away parts of myself, willingly, to keep him happy. I saw that, after that relationship ended. And vowed, again, to never to do that again.

And yet I did, with Mr. Europe. There I was... giving myself away... unconsciously. In ever more subtle ways, but still the same pattern.

What for?

For love.

For security.

For acceptance.

To avoid conflict. To avoid upsetting someone. To avoid being bullied. To avoid being yelled at.

People pleaser.

Keep people happy, and you'll be safe.

It's a valid way to interact with the world IF you have no power.

But people pleasing and power are mutually exclusive. Your primary focus is either to keep everyone around you happy, or to stay true to yourself, no matter what.

Staying true requires power. Or bestows power. Or maybe both. But it means that people can't fuck with you. They can't control you. They can't own you. They have to respect you and play by your rules.

In Lion's Gate Hospital Acute Psych Ward, I was not a people pleaser. It was the Rebel blazing in my heart. She's the one who carried me through that situation and all the way through to healing and recovery.

For that I am grateful. She's been with me the whole time – maybe she's a guardian angel, maybe she's an archetype, maybe she's a past life, maybe she's a psychological construct. It all depends on the lens you use to look.

It doesn't matter though.

What matters is the function she performed for me. What matters is how she protected me, and guided me, and brought me safely to this place.

What matters is that her energy is available to each and every one of us. Anyone can call up the energy of the Rebel Heart Warrior in their lives when they need it.

She's the one who stands up to the Gestapo. She's the one who shelters slaves on the Underground Railway. She's the one who cuts down the Conscientious Objector, tied to a post on the battlefield, in full view of the army and dares them to shoot her.

The Rebel Heart Warrior knows what's real and what's true and isn't afraid to stand up for it – even at the risk of her own life.

She stands up for it because she knows that how we live is more important than avoiding death. She stands up because she knows that the flame of the Rebel lives inside every heart. And the blaze of truth in one heart can set another heart afire, and another heart, and another heart after that.

The Rebel reminds us that we don't have to please other people, we don't have to fit in, and we don't have to believe the dominant construct of our culture. She reminds us that to be in service to Truth, is to be in service to life.

And fuck anyone who wants to deny, bury or suppress the Truth.

Because it's the truth that will set us free.

And that is me now.

Free.

I'm free of that diagnosis of bipolar disorder handed out to me in 2004 at Lion's Gate Hospital. I'm free of those two experiences of psychosis. I'm free even of that deep yearning for home.

I've made it.

I am home.

I am.

The sun is again shining in my life, so THERE!

* * *

Acknowledgements

Laingholm, 2018

I made it.

And so did this book.

Today, the day I send the final manuscript to my publisher, it is fourteen years to the week since I walked out of Lion's Gate Hospital's Acute Psych Ward for the first time. That moment when I realised my life had changed forever.

Fourteen years is half a Saturn cycle – it takes Saturn between 27 to 29 years to travel through our natal chart. My awakening / psychosis happened right on my Saturn Returns. Astrology geeks, like my friend Melissa Billington will know exactly what that means. So let's start the acknowledgements there, with Melissa. She has walked this path beside me for over a decade, as a friend, a teacher, a fellow Awakener and the godmother to my son, Sam. Thank you Melissa, for the way in which you constantly show up for me. Melissa was one of my proofreaders, along with Rama Wharerimu. He is a brand new friend on this path of awakening, but already inner circle. Like so many of my amazing friends, Rama and I met at a party, and talked and danced into the night. Thank you Rama for your encouragement and support!

I'm pausing now, to look out the window and up at the cloud-filled sky. Alex Cruz's latest *Deep & Sexy* playlist streams through my speaker. And I'm sitting at a two-tiered desk with space for my altar and my computer, one on each level. This is my sacred space and my working space, although everything is sacred. The desk sits in my bedroom with it's peaked ceiling and pentagram light fixture, double wardrobes and French doors leading out on to the back deck. This is my dream bedroom, and this is my dream home.

Sam and I finally found the family home we were dreaming about over lunch with my Mum last December. We moved into the three-bedroom, open-plan rental in April with our beautiful flatmate Rebecca. The back deck looks out over the Waitakere Ranges, which start where our backyard ends. Yes, I have a forest in my backyard. And if I look southwest, there are water views of Manukau Harbour. This is our home and we love it.

This home has held me this week, with the ocean and the forest and the fire in the lounge, as my heart has cracked open again, further, deeper, wider… a final initiation of the memoir process. Through this period, so many people have supported me, encouraged me, loved me and been there for me.

The walls around my heart have been dismantled and I am surrounded by a community of friends who love and care for me deeply. People like Helen, Toni, Jase, Matiu, Nik, Connie, Jay, Rā, Emma, Pip, and Nick. These people understand my heart and I could call any of them day or night for whatever I needed. We have each other's backs and that feels fucking good.

Back to the book, because there are more people involved in the creation of this book, like my beta-readers, Sarah and Crystal. Thank you for pouring over that third draft and providing detailed and astute feedback. And thank you to my final, final proofer, Renee Meiklejohn who is not only an eagle-eyed schoolteacher but also one of my oldest friends. We met in 1995 after I'd dropped out of Auckland University, when I landed a job waitressing at The Sandbar in Takapuna. Renee showed me the hospo ropes. We partied together and then moved in together, and started working bars in town and hitting up Showgirls when we were done working. We made it sister! We fucking made it, all the way from slinging drinks to slinging yoga mats, because Renee is a yoga teacher now too.

This book would never have become what it is without the deft touch of my editor, Feet Banks. He turned around the final draft in a stupidly tight timeframe, playing hooky from his day job to get it done, and he did it all with jokes and smiles. Especially anal jokes. Yep, he's the reason that chapter made it into the book. Feet insisted that every great book contains anal sex, just like every great relationship.

Feet's care and love was all the more potent because he was in Whistler when everything went down. That's when we met and became friends... he was a waiter at Sushi Village and responsible for serving Mr. Australia and I litres of hot sake a couple times a week. So Feet knew everybody in the Whistler portion of the story, and everything that happened. Except maybe the anal sex. He didn't know about that, until I mentioned it in passing... and then wham bam thank you ma'am, we have an entire chapter on it. Feet, I love you, you're amazing, and let's do this again. Although I won't be able to promise anal sex next time.

Of all the men I've loved... Pete Longworth will always hold a special place in my heart. We made a pact one night when we we sat up talking until 7am to never become physically intimate with each other, despite our great love. And we've stuck to it – even when I deliberately pushed the boundaries one week on the Gold Coast... so much love and respect to you Pete! Pete taught me how to be emotionally vulnerable with a man, and he photographed my process of stepping back into trance state. I call him the world's best photographer because... he is. His work is artistry on the visual plane, and magic on the astral plane. Pete knows exactly how to draw out the truth and heart of everyone he shoots because he sees the beauty in every moment. Every single moment. What a gift.

I give thanks to all the men that I have walked with on the path of relationship. I love you all, and I am grateful for the mirror that each of you held up to me at different stages of my evolution. And I acknowledge that depending on when we loved each other... that I would have caused pain and hurt because of my unskillfulness in holding other people's hearts. Hell, I didn't even know my own heart until the last decade... I was not capable of caring for other people's! Thank you, each of you, for the love and the learning and the gifts that you brought into my life. Bowing, with gratitude.

Finally, I want to thank my family, because I know that this journey hasn't been easy for them either. Hell, I'm not easy for them. I made my sister's life a misery when she was a child and teenager, yet she never held it against me and has always loved me. Lori-Ellen, you are the most extraordinary sister that I could have, and I am so proud of the woman you've become. My brother and his wife were there in Whistler with me for a few years, and they have supported me in so many small and large ways, like lending me money when I came home to New Zealand. Kendall and Celeste, just knowing I could always call on you meant so much. And yes, Kendall, I promise that I'll get Ryan Reynolds to play you in the movie. I'm not sure he does you justice though!

Dad, thank you for your support over the years, even when you didn't understand what I was going through and what it was all about. We made it in the end, and that's something to cherish.

And to my Mum... who I was unconsciously so fucking angry at for all those years... thank you for your unwavering love through those difficult times when I shut you out. You never once retaliated with anger of your own. You just held the loving-line, trusting that I would eventually work it all out, which I did. You were brave enough to begin this work of unfold and unravelling in your thirties and forties. This laid the foundation that I built on, all these years later. You are a pioneer and I love you very much. We've broken the chain of destruction in our maternal line and we can celebrate that!

It's raining again now, even though the sky through my window still shows blue. Such is life here in the rainforest. The sun shines, even when it rains. Perfection abounds. Pete just called to congratulate me and honour me. Which made me cry of course. That man has stunning timing. There he is, in the States somewhere... and he calls, just as I put the final touches on his paragraph.

But of course he did. That's our connection. And that's unity consciousness, right there.

That is love.

It abounds.

Shine on.

Author Bio

Born and raised in New Zealand, Kara-Leah is an internationally-renowned author, retreat leader, and teacher. She has impacted millions of people over the last decade through her articles, books, videos and teaching. Passionate about liberation in this lifetime, Kara-Leah practices and teaches an every day path of awakening - the path of the Awakened Heart Warrior. This path is grounded in Tantra and focuses on dissolving layers of the conditioned mind into deeper and deeper heart-felt presence. Kara-Leah's work, through her teaching, writing and retreats, focuses on using the process of compassionate inquiry to reveal conditioned mind, and so help people to drop down into being-ness and presence. She is the author of two previous books, *Forty Days of Yoga* and *The No-More-Excuses Guide to Yoga*. She can often be found dancing in her living room with her son for no reason at all.

Find her here: http://karaleah.com/

Forty Days of Yoga

You feel better when you practice yoga daily. You're calmer, stronger, more flexible and life has more ease. You're connected and in-tune. You *know* this and yet it's still almost impossible to get on your mat and practice. There's always a reason *why not*.

Not have enough time. Not the right space. Not enough knowledge of postures or sequences. Not disciplined enough. Not enough willpower. *Not, not, not!*

But is this really TRUE? *Forty Days of Yoga* takes you on a journey to examine what *really* stops you from practicing yoga.

This book shifts your mindset and gives you the tools you need to create and maintain a home yoga practice. It's not a book – it's a result. And *that* is gold.

Find out how to design strategies to make daily practice possible in your life – no matter what your life is like. And discover that you *already* have the time, space, willpower, discipline and know-how to create and maintain your home yoga practice.

All you've been missing is the single-pointed focus and clear strategy to make it happen.

This is not a one-size fits all solution – this is a journey into your mind that helps you tease out *your* personal reasons for blocking or sabotaging your home yoga practice. Your ideal home yoga practice is about what *you need and what works with your* lifestyle.

Nothing will get in the way of you and your home yoga practice again. It will just be a part of who you are and what you do.

All you have to do… is buy the book.

Find it in all good books stores or on Amazon here: https://www.amazon.com/Forty-Days-Yoga-Kara-Leah-Grant/dp/0473239582.

The No-More-Excuses Guide to Yoga

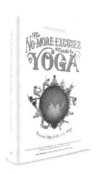

I t's time to bust some yoga myths with Kara-Leah Grant, yoga teacher, writer and trusted ally. *The No-More-Excuses Guide to Yoga* shows you that yoga IS for everybody.

It's the essential companion guide on your journey to brilliant heath and well-being.

Clear, no nonsense and easy to follow, you'll find all the answers to your burning yoga questions:

- Which class is right for me?

- How do I stretch myself and keep my body safe?

- What if I can't understand the instructions in class?

- Could my body react in an embarrassing way?

- Do I need a new yoga path?

- Is my teacher right for me?

- How can I motivate myself to practice consistently?

Kara-Leah Grant has designed and written this book just for you as the ultimate yoga companion.

With in-depth instruction on how to choose the best yoga path, style, teacher and studio for your lifestyle, you'll easily overcome all the excuses that may be preventing you from getting to class.

Available in all good book stores or in Amazon here: https://www.amazon.com/No-More-Excuses-Guide-Yoga-Because-Every-ebook/dp/B00S8P918Q/.

Made in the
USA
Middletown, DE